The
Rainbow
Onion

The Transformative Power of Color Thinking

MAGGIE HUFFMAN

Ebook: ISBN: 978-1-7351777-0-0

Print: ISBN: 978-1-7351777-1-7

TheRainbowOnion.com

*I lovingly dedicate this to **all** the people who create ripples by throwing a better version of themselves into the world on a daily basis. Splash!*

TABLE OF CONTENTS

GRAB THE FREE RESOURCES!

TheRainbowOnion.com™

Throughout the book, you'll find references to bonus material that will help you get the most out of this book and *The Rainbow Onion* process. These are things like worksheets, fun and beautiful color samples, reference material, and videos.

Here's how it works: You give me your email; I send you stuff. The first thing I send you is login information to a special website section with links to the bonus material. Once a week, you'll also get an email with a blog post, and then maybe some occasional offers. Check it out. You can unsubscribe at any time... but I hope you'll stay!

You can access bonus material here:

www.therainbowonion.com/bonus

Introduction

What Is This Color Thinking Stuff?

"A book is a dream that you hold in your hand."

Neil Gaiman

I chose the quote above because you hold *The Rainbow Onion* in your hand. I believe you chose this book because you have a dream. Whatever your dream is, there is a good chance Color Thinking will help you realize it. But you have questions, right? Let's get you some answers!

The purpose of *The Rainbow Onion* is to take you on a journey of transformation, which means there will be stuff for you to do. This book is chewy. That means you'll read a chunk and chew on it—put the book down, think a little, write a bit, do some stuff, and come back to bite off another chunk. How big are the bites? How fast will you chew? All up to you, my friend.

Q&A

I bet you're wondering about all the basics—who, what, when, where, and why. I would be, because I'm naturally curious, but also because I'm wired to be a questioner. I like to establish a few facts before I invest effort in exploring something new. Let me take a stab at some Q&As right up front.

Why Color?

People love color. It's an integral part of the sense of sight. It's made of light.

Pretty much everyone has a relationship with color. We are surrounded by color. Most of us have a favorite color or two or three; and a color or two we detest. Colors can evoke emotions and memories. Colors can surprise us with their intensity. Some colors are calming and soothe us, while some colors repel us.

Color is also a language—a profound language. As with any language, there are nuances and dialects and differences. Throughout history, humans have used color to communicate. We have given colors all kinds of meanings: Spiritual, symbolic, personal, emotional, and more.

This language of color is very complex. There is no single meaning associated with any one color. There are levels and layers to our usage and understanding of the language of color, as with any language.

We can use this color information to engineer our own personal transformations.

How Did Color Thinking and The Rainbow Onion Come to Be?

I have always always always loved color and light. I collect colors, especially the vibrant ones. I am as distracted by a bright color as my dog is by a squirrel. I love to be surrounded by light and crystals and any kind of refracting or reflecting surfaces because I love the spectrum of color as much as I love any individual color. I believe the answer to the question "more glitter?" is always "yes," because glitter is color *and* light!

My favorite color is purple, and it always has been—in pretty much any shade or hue—though for a very long time I didn't understand why. Now I do.

When I got a job working in the art department for a calendar and greeting card company, I was in heaven, because in that job I learned so much about color theory and communicating intentionally with color. I also got to play with the best art toys. And I got paid! I mixed my own colors when I painted, so I could understand how they were made and their relationships to each other.

I moved on to do a lot of other things professionally, which I'll refer to at times, but I'm not going to bore you with listing all of those. Let's just skip over many years and say my careers have created a colorful patchwork quilt of experiences. But my nerdy love of colors does have a purpose in this story, so let's get back to it.

About fifteen years ago, I had my first Aura-Soma session. I'm going to reserve the details for when I tell more of that story in a couple of pages, but it was my introduction to color as a tool for self-understanding and as a healing modality. I realized then that I wanted to become a healer in some capacity.

I completed a lot of trainings and certifications. I became an Aura-Soma Practitioner. I became an Integrative Health Coach. I became a certified Life Coach. I earned a second Master's degree. I was in the middle of becoming a certified Master Life Coach when I said, "Enough!" (Actually, I had to be told, which is a story for another time! And I had some other issues with the school, but that, too, is another story.)

I started playing with Color Thinking. I started using specific colors with my individual clients and in my master coaching group, and the results were amazing. I realized I had access to all the things I needed to bring a color system together and share it. *The Rainbow Onion* was born. It started out as a set of tools, but very quickly showed up as much more. Color Thinking is a process for personal transformation, with a whole lot of built-in support.

For me, writing this book and introducing *The Rainbow Onion* to the world as a system for Color Thinking is a calling. Everything has been leading up to this.

What Does The Rainbow Onion Mean?

Life, life coaching, and any kind of transformation are like onions. Just when you think you've mastered something, another layer appears. And every time you peel down to a new layer, the next layer is fresh and intense. Very often, there are tears, because of the intensity of the experience.

Rainbows appear when the sun (light) comes out after the cleansing rain (like tears). Rainbows include all the colors; so rainbows are a sign of diversity and acceptance. Rainbows symbolize the promise of hope and trust. Rainbows are a sign of transformation.

Throughout time, groups of people have chosen the rainbow as their symbol precisely because of everything the spectrum of colors represents. In the Judeo-Christian tradition, rainbows represent God's promise. In the 1960s, a rainbow flag stood for world peace. Today, it is a symbol of acceptance and pride for the LGBTQ+ community. In the spring of 2020, during the Covid-19 lockdown in Italy, the rainbow was adopted as a symbol that everything would be alright, *"andra tutto bene."*

Also, onions make almost anything taste better.

I chose the name *The Rainbow Onion* for this system for *all* of the above reasons.

Who Is This For?

The Rainbow Onion program is for anyone who wants help with a personal transformation or change, confirmation of being on the right path, or support for staying on that path. All that's required is an open mind, an open heart, and a willingness to be honest with yourself. Transformation doesn't have to be hard!

You don't have to be super woo-woo or New Age, but it doesn't hurt. *The Rainbow Onion* program doesn't replace any religion or science or therapeutic beliefs or school of thought. You can totally pick the parts of the program you want to use because there's no one-size-fits-all anything. There are no rules, only hints and guidelines. You don't have to give up anything or go it alone. In fact, *The Rainbow Onion* is better with friends.

Whether you treat *The Rainbow Onion* as a bunch of concepts, some stories, a program, a practice, or whatever else, it helps you access your own creativity. You open yourself to layers of meaning and understanding. You connect more deeply to the world around you, as you see and feel connections. You access a whole lot more support than you might have guessed was out there for you.

And, Finally, Why Now?

I believe we are at a unique point in history. We have never been so polarized, so divided as we are today. There is an epidemic of binary thinking, of reducing things to black or white, good or bad, right or wrong.

There is also a literal pandemic going on as I write this. As humans, we have had a variety of responses. I can't begin to guess how it will unfold, but I do know this: The world needs healing. The world needs less pain.

We can start by transforming our own lives to become the best versions of ourselves. The world needs us to be our best. I believe in the ripple effect. That's how we make a better world.

I guess I'm being called—right now—to toss a colorful onion into the pot and see how big a splash it will make.

How and Why to Use This Book

When I first started writing books, I learned there are books called "airplane reads". They are crafted to be short and simple enough to read and digest on a cross-country flight, so read in four to five hours. Short, simple, concise, and focused are all qualities to be admired. This book *ain't* that. Sure, you might be able to skim through it on a long flight if you're a fast reader, but you won't digest the book in that amount of time.

I could tell you that you must read the book cover to cover, but we both know I can't make you do anything. So why don't I give you a few suggestions on how to use this book based on what YOU hope to get out of it. Now, there's a novel approach, right? (Okay, okay. I know this doesn't count as a novel.)

Why were you attracted to this book?

Were you attracted because you want some kind of healing or transformation, and you intuitively know color can help? Because you are craving color? Because you were mysteriously drawn? Or maybe you accidentally found the book, but now the idea of using color is pretty interesting. If any of those reasons fit, I suggest you go all in. Read the book and work the exercises as you go. Read a chapter, then pause to do the exercise at the end before you move on to the next chapter. Let the process unfold in layers.

Did you see the name of the book and become curious? Does anything about color pique your curiosity? Awesome. You probably want to read and maybe dabble with the exercises. Ideally, you'd read the book from cover to cover, absolutely enthralled. But I know—life happens. Shiny objects really do happen.

I suggest reading Part 1 to get a feel for what Color Thinking is all about. See if you can apply it to something important to you now. Do as much or as little as you want now. You'll be back. You'll see.

Are you fascinated by a specific color? Has it been stalking you, leaving you signs and love notes all over? Are you looking for confirmation that you understand the message about why you're noticing it everywhere? You might want to skip around in the book. You can go to the appendix and research that specific color, though reading Part 1 will probably also be helpful. You can go to *The Rainbow Onion* website to get more details and resources for any specific color:

therainbowonion.com/bonus.

I've written this book to share the complicated stuff, but you can use Color Thinking in less complicated ways as well. You can use it on the spot (that's a printing pun) in a targeted way—just to think differently about a specific situation. You can use Color Thinking like you would use oracle or tarot cards—to show you what you need to know, to confirm your intuition and to help you think in a more aligned way. In Chapter 15, I'll show you some examples of how to do that.

I've thrown a lot of content into this book. Keep what you want, toss the rest. You can change your life in a way you might not yet believe is possible by using this material. But you will (believe, that is). You'll see.

At the end of each chapter, there are two sections: A Color Thinking story and an exercise.

The first section, the Color Thinking story, is a real-life story of how someone (usually a client) has experienced Color Thinking and how it impacted their transformation. Stories are so much easier to digest than theoretical explanations. Most of the stories are revealed in layers. One chapter's story might focus on color, another on thinking, until it's pulled together.

The second section is an exercise for you to do—if you choose. This section will have all the instructions you need. You might want to get a journal and some colorful writing implements so you can get really creative and expressive. Or you might want to take advantage of the resources I've bundled for you as bonus content. I've created worksheets, activities, images, and other formats, so you can print, watch, fill-in, use them as reference, etc. In many cases, they are the same worksheets I use in Rainbow Onion workshops.

As you'll see very soon, I am not a fan of either/or thinking. So why not do both? —grab the bonus content AND express yourself creatively. Color outside the lines, even. Gasp!

If you want the bonuses (come on! they're free!), you'll need to go to the website **therainbowonion.com/bonus** and sign up. You'll get immediate access to the bonus material. You'll have to give me your email, but I think that's a pretty fair exchange. I'll send you my weekly blog post, and also the odd additional email now and then. You can unsubscribe any time you want—but I hope you'll stick around!

What to Expect and What's Next

There are no accidents. You will start seeing signs and symbols all over the place. There will be these mythical things called coincidences surrounding you. You'll notice them. Pay attention. Use them.

You can also expect layers. You'll think you've finished one thing, only to discover there's something else underneath. Don't worry, that's a good thing. The layers take us deeper and deeper into the human experience.

There may be tears. How lucky is that? Tears are cleansing. Tears are expressive. I used to think crying was something to avoid unless I was alone. I had to get over it because my eyes had a very different agenda. I would be at work, and pretty much any time I felt something intense (commitment, passion, joy, empathy, anger, frustration) my face would start leaking. I decided it wasn't worth being self-conscious about, and if I didn't have a problem with it, no one else needed to, either. I was in a male-dominated industry, company, and role—and it still worked—so there went my stereotypes! Tears are emotions leaking out through the cracks in our mask so the pressure doesn't cause us to explode.

You are a beautiful, colorful onion, intense and layered. You make everything better. Of course there will be tears—you are powerful stuff. Fantastic!

Color Thinking Story – The Colors I Chose

I mentioned a few pages ago that I had my first Aura-Soma session about ten years ago and was introduced to the idea of a new healing modality. I also learned more about healing during that session.

There was a time in my life when I thought healing meant treating an illness or disease. That's an accurate description of healing in a medical context, when the body might need help. But that's not the kind of healing I'm talking about here.

You see, I don't start with the belief that we are broken or diseased or sick. We don't need to be "fixed." But we can always be growing, evolving, and becoming better versions of ourselves. That's the New Age definition of healing, I guess—becoming more whole in body, mind and spirit—and that's the kind of healing I'm talking about in this context of color and *The Rainbow Onion*.

Back to my story. About fifteen years ago, I ran into something called Aura-Soma. I had no idea what it was. Someone I really trusted (okay, it was my mom) recommended it. She told me it was the best, most amazing thing ever, but she couldn't describe it. I went with her to Elizabeth's house.

Elizabeth is this tall, beautiful woman with gorgeously wild, curly hair. She has a personality, and a heart, as big as the sky. Elizabeth is many things, including an intuitive and an Aura-Soma practitioner. She told us we were going to do a consult, but we would start with a guided meditation. We did, which was totally amazing.

When we got to the consult, she showed us a cabinet of beautiful bottles of color. Each bottle had two colors—what, how? I later learned that the bottles were made of up both an oil-based and a water-based faction. The oil floats in the upper half of the bottle, on top of the water. The oil can be one color and the water can be another. Presto, each bottle can have two different colors in it!

Most importantly, the colors are really pretty. Vivid. Entrancing. The colors in each bottle shine like jewels. You can't help but *ooh* and *ahh* when you see them.

When it came time for my consult, Elizabeth had me choose four bottles. Her instructions were to choose the bottles using my intuition, based on which ones shone or sang out to me, and to pay attention to the order in which I chose them.

I picked my four bottles, and what I learned was truly life changing. There is a universal language of color, and there are cultural and personal meanings that each of us overlay on top of these meanings. As Elizabeth and I explored each bottle, based on the order in which I had chosen them, and the messages of the colors in the top and bottom factions, something big shifted for me. I understood things about myself that I didn't understand before, much less believed. As I decided to take a bottle and work with it, Elizabeth told me, "You are the colors you choose."

I worked with that bottle and had profound experiences, mostly learning about myself and my talents. I went back a couple of months later to do another consult. When I saw the bottles again, I had the same kid-in-a-candy-store reaction—they were so beautiful. As I gushed about how gorgeous the bottles of color were, Elizabeth again said, "You are the colors you choose."

I had another awesome consult and took a bottle home to work with, and again I had a huge personal growth spurt. (And yes, there were growing pains.)

The third time I went back...same story. Fast forward to Elizabeth saying, again, "You are the colors you choose," and I finally got it. The bottles are so beautiful. I am the colors I choose. *I am beautiful*. For a smart girl, I felt quite slow.

I learned a whole lot more from Aura-Soma, the colors and Elizabeth. But really, truly coming to know and believe I was beautiful—I had a beautiful soul and it could be seen—was such a profound change for me. I felt like I had been introduced to the real me for the first time. It also profoundly changed the way I "worked on myself." I no longer approached myself as a huge to-do list of DIY projects i.e. things to fix. I started believing in the things I was good at, in my own special gifts and talents, and also believing that they lined up with the things I loved.

That's what I mean by healing. It's not *fixing*, but *becoming*. This was the start of a fantastic journey to become a better version of myself. I came to understand myself better. By now, I have updated my beliefs to reflect who I want to be and to serve me to become that person. Because I began working with color, I got to go deeper and make a bigger difference in my world.

That's why I am sharing this with you.

Color Thinking Exercise – Your Relationship Conversation

Your first exercise is to begin to play with your own relationship with color—because you do have a relationship. You're likely gonna need to have one of *those* conversations. You know: "We need to talk about our *relationship*." Don't make it weird. Make it fun! Talk amongst yourself.

Think about your answers to the questions below and write down the answers. You might want to pick a colorful journal and writing implements. You know, invest a little in the relationship.

What is your relationship with color? Do you know? Explore it.

- How would you describe your relationship with color?
- How much do you think about color?
- How big a part of your life is color?
- Where could you add in MORE color in your life?
- What is a story about you and a color?
- What's your favorite color? Why?
- What does your favorite color remind you of?
- How does your favorite color make you feel?
- What are some powerful memories you have involving your favorite color?
- What's your least favorite color? Why?
- How does your least favorite color make you feel?

***

You now have some of the *Who, What, When, Where,* and *Why* questions about Color Thinking and *The Rainbow Onion* answered, but I know more questions are going to come up. After you've spent some time tending to your relationship with color, we'll move on to Part 1 and dig into the next layer.

PART 1

COLOR + THINKING = COLOR THINKING

"What we can say for sure is that the language of color is tricky. Children who can discern the difference between a triangle and a square with ease may still struggle differentiating pink from red or orange. We also know that not having a separate word for something does not mean we can't distinguish it."

–Kassia St. Clair

Part 1 is the foundational teaching part of this book. It contains three chapters that build upon each other (you know, layers) and gives you everything you need to know about how the components of Color Thinking come together so that you can start using *The Rainbow Onion* process in Part 2. We start with building an understanding of color, layer on an understanding of how we think, and then put them together to make Color Thinking. In Part 1, we will be working on building your color vocabulary. We'll start in Chapter 1, and you'll continue to build by adding layers in the next two chapters.

What's in Part 1

Chapter 1 – Introductions are for introducing. Chapters are for diving into the detail. In the introduction, I introduced the idea that color is a language. In this chapter, I'm going to explain a lot more about how color works, how color is one of many languages, and how universal, yet personal, it is. In this chapter—and in the companion workbook, which you can get online at **therainbowonion.com/bonus**—you'll start to build your own color vocabulary.

Chapter 2 – To understand thinking, you need to know a bit about current neuroscience and coaching concepts. There are a ton of myths and misconceptions out there, and we wanna bust them, especially those that make things seem difficult. This section sets you up to successfully and easily work through *The Rainbow Onion* process.

Chapter 3 – We know about black and white thinking, but what is this Color Thinking stuff? What are some patterns that could be keeping us stuck? Let me list a few. And while I'm at it, why don't I count off some of the *ways* and *whys* I'm loving Color Thinking? And if I'm brave enough, I'll even get around to a definition of what Color Thinking actually is...

CHAPTER 1

THE SCIENCE AND LANGUAGE OF COLOR

"...if 'colour' is intimately bound up with language—if it is a system of arbitrary signs—it must also be a function of culture and have its own history."

–John Gage, Color and Meaning

Color is not only intimately bound up with language, it is also bound up with culture, history, and ultimately with our own perceptions of color.

Colors are a very profound language for us. Color Thinking is thinking in a different language in order to see things from a different perspective. We'll get to Color Thinking in depth later, but first I want to build the foundation of understanding color and how we can use it as a language.

What Is Color?

We all pretty much know what color is, but just to make sure we start off on the same page, I'm going to give us a few common points of definition.

In doing the research for this section, I discovered there are a lot of definitions, and they vary greatly based on one's perspective. For example, artists have a different definition than physicists. I thought about including all the technical stuff about color here, but I realized if you were interested in that, you would have bought a different book. and it would just make me look even geekier than I am. Besides, if you want to find out about it, you have access to Google and Wikipedia.

I decided to default to a very reliable source to explain what color is. You're welcome. According to Crayola, one of my very first resources for playing with color:

"Color is the aspect of things that is caused by differing qualities of light being reflected or emitted by them. To see color, you have to have light. When light shines on an object some colors bounce off the object and others are absorbed by it. Our eyes only see the colors that are bounced off or reflected.

The sun's rays contain all the colors of the rainbow mixed together. This mixture is known as white light. When white light strikes a white crayon or marker barrel, it appears white to us because it absorbs no color and reflects all color equally. A black crayon or marker cap absorbs all colors equally and reflects none, so it looks black to us. While artists consider black a color, scientists do not because black is the absence of all color.

All light rays contain color. Light is made of electromagnetic waves. These waves spread out from any light source, such as the sun. Light waves travel at tremendous speed (186,000 miles or 300,000 kilometers per second). Different colors have different wavelengths, which is the distance between corresponding parts of two of the waves. The longest wavelength of light that humans can see is red. The shortest is violet. Ultraviolet has an even shorter wavelength, but humans cannot see it. Some birds and bees can see ultraviolet light. Infrared has a longer wavelength than red light, and humans cannot see this light but can feel the heat infrared generates."

(Source: www.crayola.com/for-educators/resources-landing/articles/color-what-is-color.aspx)

I like that definition because it conveniently includes all the points I want to make, but in a much more concise and sciencey-sounding way than I could have done. Just to be a bit repetitive and redundant, let me pull out a couple of the key points:

1. Color is light being reflected by a physical object.
2. White light is a mixture of all the colors of the rainbow reflected back to us.
3. All light contains color.
4. Light is made up of electromagnetic waves (which are caused by vibrations).
5. We can feel color, even when we cannot see it.

These things are all scientific facts, yet they sound like New Age stuff. They could even be understood and unpacked as full of theological symbolism, right?

This compels me to make a confession. I need to confess that I have another bias. I think like a scientist AND I believe in magic. I don't see a contradiction there. I believe magic is made up of things science cannot explain... yet. So, you will see me slip and slide quite comfortably between magic and science. I hope you feel free to join me.

Oh, one other thing. The science of color is primarily about studying the perception of color. We can explain how color is created (refracting light waves that aren't absorbed by an object) and know that color is a physical thing that is detected by the retina in our eyes, but it is interpreted in the brain—and while we humans have made amazing progress understanding our brains, we have a long way to go before we can fully explain what goes on in there, especially when it comes to perception and interpretation.

The Rainbow Onion is an extension of color science, in that we will be studying how we perceive, translate, interpret, and experience color, and how we can use it to make our lives more meaningful.

The Language of Color

I mentioned in the Introduction that *The Rainbow Onion* process views color as a language. A language is, simply put, a way to communicate. We use color to communicate; ergo, it's a language. Simple logic. Not such a simple language.

We communicate many things through the use of color, and we respond to color on many levels: Viscerally, emotionally and intellectually, to name just a few. We infer meaning based upon our responses to color.

Sometimes our use of color is intentional, like when we choose colors, or our words about colors, carefully. Some intentional examples of this are choosing colors for a brand, a room, a flower, an outfit, or a gift. Other times, we communicate about colors subconsciously. For example, we might choose a color just because it makes us feel a certain way, without being aware of our rationale.

As with any language, there are cultural influences, regional dialects, individual nuances, and other differences in how the language is used and interpreted. Throughout history, as humans have used color to communicate, we have built up lexicons of color meaning in layers: Spiritual, symbolic, personal, emotional, and more.

Yes, this language of color is very complex. There is no single meaning associated with any one color. There are levels and layers to our usage and understanding of the language of color, as with any language. While we often want to try to simplify things down to their essence, it would not serve us here to distill each color down to a single, common definition. The beauty of color as a language is in the richness, the complexity, and the depth of its meaning.

Let's look at some of these layers, or levels, to begin to understand the interplay—because, yes, we get to play with colors!

Universal

One level of the color language is pretty universal, based on common human experience. We associate some colors directly with the things in the world that are that color (sunshine, bodies of water, grassy fields, forests and trees, weather events, flowers, fruit and foods, etc.) and the relationship these things have with our life force. This level is part of an energetic language –since color is light, color is vibration. For example, yellow is associated with sunlight, and because of this, it evokes joy, warmth, and happiness. Many people paint their kitchens a shade of yellow so they will feel bright and cheerful. (Don't worry, we will get into a lot more detail as we go. That was just one example.)

Cultural

Another level of the color language is symbolic, which can be heavily influenced by our culture. Colors can have very different meanings from one culture to another. Let's take yellow again. In Western culture, as in the Old West of North America, yellow was associated with cowardice ("Why, you yellow-bellied lizard," said the Colorado cowboy in a slow drawl.) But in Japanese culture yellow represents courage. Yellow has also been a symbol of persecution for Jews, as seen in European history. Archeologists have researched what yellow meant in ancient cultures. How fascinating to think about what yellow meant in ancient Mayan culture, right?

And, of course, as individuals we can connect multiple cultural or regional influences to colors. We could have parents from different cultures, or we may have moved around the world. Either would create a multi-cultural color influence. This is not getting simpler, is it? Just wait. There's more!

Personal

Another level is our own personal color history. This is unique because it's based on our life experiences, events, and memories—each of which includes an emotional memory. Think again about yellow. What does yellow mean to *you*? What's the very first thing you think of when you think of the color yellow? Does yellow remind you of sunshine and flowers? The color of your mother's hair? A dress you wore in the summer during high school years? The color of your kitchen in your first apartment? Is yellow one of your favorite colors?

Understanding your personal color vocabulary—what colors say to you and what you try to convey with colors—is a vital, enlightening, and fun part of the practice of *The Rainbow Onion*... and it's a great place to start. At the end of this chapter, you'll find a link to some exercises to help you define and document your color vocabulary.

Symbolic

When color is used to represent something specific—like a material object—or to invoke an abstract concept or emotion, it is being used symbolically. Here's an example: Yellow is often used to convey caution or danger, and so it is used with traffic lights, emergency vehicles, and caution signs. This makes sense because yellow is a bright color, is highly reflective, and the human eye processes yellow light first.

Yellow is one of the colors used in safety wear, often called high-vis clothing, because of its combination of being readily visible and its symbolic meaning of caution.

That's a pretty straight-forward example, but there are also more complex examples of using color for symbolic meaning. Symbolism usually is complex. I bet you have your own symbolic meanings for colors. You'll be using those to build your own color lexicon.

Spiritual

We cannot forget the spiritual layer. Color is part of almost every spiritual tradition. In fact, I can't find an exception. Color has a long history of being used to communicate meaning and symbolism in spiritual practices. The amount of scholarship out there is staggering, as archeologists, art historians, theologians, and others have set out to interpret—and reinterpret—spiritual associations of color.

Colors are used to represent religious or spiritual concepts, such as purity, innocence, redemption, and love. They are used in décor and vestments. They're also used to communicate hierarchy in an organization, and seasons in a liturgical calendar. Colors are used extensively in the art of most religious traditions.

Colors are used to represent different types of spiritual energy in chakra systems, auras and energy healing.

Color combinations are used to identify specific religious orders.

Specific entities, such as archangels, angels, ascended masters, saints' days, and even deities can have an association with a specific color. Here are a few examples: Archangel Rafael is often associated with blue, ascended master Hilarion is associated with green, the Hindu goddess Parvati is golden, Krishna has a blue aura, and there's a Yellow Emperor in China.

I don't need to add volumes to the content already out there. What's important is to know there is a spiritual element to the language of color. For you it may come from your culture or religious tradition, or it may come from your own personal experiences.

For me, the spiritual aspect of color—how my spirit uses color—shows up through creativity. We are mirrors of creation; some would say of the Creator. When we create, when we are creative, we are the best and truest reflection. So, to me, the idea of using color as a language of creative expression is a spiritual experience. It's a layer of my Rainbow Onion.

Balance: The Spectrum Within a Color

When I studied to become an Aura-Soma Practitioner, I was introduced to the idea that colors have both positive messages or meanings (gifts) and messages that are often interpreted as negative (challenges). As time went on, I came to understand it isn't as simple as two polarities, a positive and a negative. There's a full *spectrum* of meaning (yes, pun intended) within any color.

I like to think of the positive, aspirational messaging as infused with light. Then there is also a darker side, the more negative and challenging messaging –a shadow side, which I think of as "saturated." The darker hues are saturated because they don't reflect as much light.

These positive and negative aspects are definitely related to each other. In fact, they define each other. If we take yellow again and place it on a spectrum, we can see an example of this relationship.

The positive, infused aspects of yellow represent sunshine, warmth, and light and evoke the emotions of joy, happiness, and bravery.

The darker, saturated, shadow aspects of yellow represent cowardice and treason and evoke the emotions of fear and persecution.

Bravery is at one end of the spectrum; fear is at the other. There are shades and degrees all along the spectrum. Joy is an antidote for fear. When you are fearful or feel persecuted, you long for the freedom from fear found in joy and happiness.

In *The Rainbow Onion*, we use balance to achieve our desired transformation. We look at the spectrum of meaning within a color to find what we need. We will go into this in greater detail in Part 2, but I wanted to introduce these two ideas—spectrum and balance—right away.

One Color, Many Meanings

The language of color is as complex as any language made of words. We use our hearts, our eyes, our memories, and our brains to communicate with color. We medicate with color— selecting colors because they make us feel a certain way. We create, heal, attract, repel, announce, and represent with color. We do so many things with color.

Color is a phenomenon and a phenomenal language. We use color to communicate our messages out to the world, be we also receive messages from the world via color. In *The Rainbow Onion*, we will mostly focus on understanding how color speaks to us in order to use it as a means to support ourselves on our paths to transformation.

All the examples above of the levels and layers of meaning in the language of color show how color is contextual. We need to understand our particular historical, cultural, and personal context to be able to decode all the secret messages colors send us.

Hmmm, that's interesting. I guess I'm saying color helps us understand ourselves, but in order to understand color, we need to understand more of ourselves. It's a bit of circular logic. Oh well. We'll just make colorful circles.

Why Color?

Ultimately, humans love color. We are attracted to colors in a visceral, powerful way. That's why color allows us to access so many parts of ourselves—our energy, our history, our culture, our beliefs, our stories, and our emotions. We can use all of this to engineer, support, and document our own personal transformations.

Confusing? Maybe. If you are looking for The One Thing—an absolute truth in black and white—then *The Rainbow Onion* isn't for you. But if you like poetry, music, complex flavor profiles, layer cake—anything with layers of meaning (or flavor), then this is a language for you!

Color Thinking Story – My Relationship with Purple

I'd like to tell you about my lifelong relationship with purple.

I'm not exactly sure when I became aware purple was my favorite color. It was pretty early on. I'm thinking... grade school? Aside from my family members, my bond with purple is my longest-running relationship.

It started with simple attraction. My eyes were always attracted to purple things. It almost didn't matter what shade they were. When I saw purple, I just felt happy.

My first understanding of a meaning of purple was that it was associated with royalty. I liked that. You see, I was 5'8" in the fifth grade—taller than my teacher. I felt like a cross between a giraffe and a palm tree—definitely something awkward that towered over the other kids. Purple, and the idea of being regal, gave me a different option, a way to think about being tall that might not be so awkward.

During my high school years, I was in pretty much every choral group I could join, including the church choir. The hymnals, choir folders, and robes were purple; so were the candles and banners during different times of the year, adding a layer of religious and spiritual meaning.

In college and grad school, my personal uniform became more and more purple. I could pretty much find ways to dress head to toe in purple

–from my hair to my converse high tops. It became my signature look until I graduated and went out into the real world to get a job.

One of my first jobs was in the art and printing world. Ironically, my signature look during that time became all black. Pre-goth era. Pre-Melbourne corporate era. I don't know what I was thinking. But everything else around me was purple! I was never a "Purple Rain" fan, though.

In 1999 I had a year of deep grief. I lost my brother, father, and grandfather within three months. One of the things that was very soothing in my grief was lavender—the color, the fragrance, the plant. For me, there is now a deep connection between the color of lavender and the fragrance, and my immediate emotional reaction is a sense of peace and familiarity, of home. I chose to name my home my Lavender Sanctuary. (I could really hop down a rabbit hole here and tell you more...)

When I studied to become an Aura-Soma practitioner, I learned the Aura-Soma system doesn't include purple; there's only violet. *Whatever...* that was my first reaction, complete with eye-roll. Okay, but there's actually a reason. Purple is made by combining the colors red and blue, and that's where all the variations in hue come from: adding a little more blue and less red or vice versa. Violet, however, is a spectral color – which means it has its own wavelength at the end of the spectrum (the blue end). Purple looks like violet to us humans, because it activates both the short and the long wave cones in our eyes. I love the idea that violet stands on its own.

I also learned violet is the color of transformation, transmutation, transfiguration, transmogrification (love that one), transition—all the trannies, as I like to think. I learned about the story of the violet flame, a spiritual energy that transmutes any negative energy into something positive. It accelerates a change of heart. The violet flame is said to be used by St. Germain, an ascended master, as a tool to deliver fast positive change.

We can also use the image of the violet flame as personal protection, by visualizing a protective bubble of violet light all around us. As anything negative approaches us, the violet flame works its alchemy and only lets in good. I love that imagery.

So, now I tend to say *violet*, but when I was younger, before my fascination with how we perceive color, I called it *purple*. The term really doesn't matter much to me.

I painted my dining room a mauve/purple color. My office walls are pale violet, and my living room is lavender. There's a place I can stand where I see all three colors at once and see the distinctions. These colors create subtle mood differences for me—intentionally—but they are all related to peace and calm. And, yes, I do have other colors in other rooms.

I tell you this story as an example of the kind of relationships we can have with colors. They grow and change over time as we keep them in our lives. And they don't need to be exclusive—I have meaningful relationships with other colors, too. It's totally cool to be polychromaticamorous!

Color Thinking Exercise – Build Your Own Color Vocabulary

Now we're going to begin building your own color vocabulary.

There are no wrong answers as you do this exercise because your answers will be based completely on your personal culture, history, perceptions, and experiences with color.

Just to remind you, as I mentioned in the Introduction, I made a worksheet for this exercise and it's available to you as bonus content. Go to **therainbowonion.com/bonus** and sign up. You'll get the password to the site so you can download the workbook and other bonus content.

To set up for this exercise, either print out the worksheet or get out your colored pencils and paper. You're going to make a table. If you're using a journal, I suggest using a couple of facing pages, so you have plenty of room to write.

In the first column of the table, on the left, write the names of the colors, writing them in that color, so you have a visual reference. Start with a list of these colors: Blue, turquoise, green, olive, yellow, orange, red, magenta, violet, pink, white, black.) You can get creative if you want about how you depict the colors—use paint chips, cut out examples from magazines. Do anything that gives you a visual example of the color.

You are going to need seven more columns as well. We'll use three of those added columns in this exercise, with these column titles: Symbols, Universal, and Cultural. (We'll get the other columns in the next two chapters.)

Once you have the table set up, work through the colors one column at a time. Look at the color (not only the name) and write down your reactions/thoughts about it in the appropriate column. Don't worry about finessing your answers. This is your vocabulary and this worksheet is for you. Your first instincts are usually the most helpful. There's no wrong answer!

Here are a few questions to get you started:

1. **Symbols** – What does this color symbolize for you? Another way to explore this is: What does this color remind you of? Make a list. For example, yellow might be "sun, daisies, lemons."
2. **Universal** – Using the info in Chapter 1 about how colors can have universal meaning based on common human experience, list some of your ideas for each color.
3. **Cultural** – In this column, list meanings that come from your specific social and cultural influences.

***

In this chapter, we explored some of the many possible layers of meanings that come in when we use color as a language. I also introduced you to the idea that there's a spectrum of meaning within a color, balancing the meanings of the shadow side and the light-infused side.

Now I hope you understand how deeply layered, complex, and personal the language of color is.

When you've done your work for this chapter—gotten a start on your own personal color vocabulary, we'll move on to Chapter 2 and explore thinking!

CHAPTER 2

THINKING

"Silence is death for any idea. An idea that is never spoken or written down dies with the person who conceived it. Ideas can only be remembered when they are repeated. They can only be believed when they are repeated."

–James Clear

In this chapter, we'll explore your brain and thinking, because the more you understand about it, the more you'll be able to manage your thinking. For some folks, the idea of managing our thinking is a very foreign concept. I'm gonna have to build my case.

Neuroscience is the mother-science of the brain, studying the structure and function of the brain. It is multidisciplinary and includes physiology, anatomy, molecular biology, biochemistry, modeling, psychology, and other behavioral sciences, to name just a few disciplines. It's the frontier of brain science.

It's also a popular topic these days. I've heard some pretty wacky statements put out there and then justified by saying, "That's neuroscience." Honestly, some people just make shit up and then justify it with pseudoscience. While it's a fun thing to do with a bunch of drunk people at a party, it sure wouldn't serve me to do that here.

I am not a neuroscientist. *Duh.* I have to rely on the experts' research and explanations to understand my brain. As in almost every other science—or human venture, for that matter—there are areas where you'll find honest people who admit there is no clear consensus, but new theories are raised and substantiated every day. What I write in this chapter will probably be outdated in a couple of years and I'll have to revise it. So, this is my CYA strategy: I may make mistakes because I'm not an expert, and because our understanding of neuroscience is incomplete and continually growing. Fine. Just so you know. In case you ARE a neuroscientist. (By the way, in corporate-speak, CYA stands for Cover Your Ass.)

But you don't have to be a neuroscientist to be able to operate your brain more effectively, just like you don't need to be a mechanical engineer to be a race car driver. You don't have to be a software developer to make magic with Photoshop, a piano manufacturer to play or compose... you get the idea. You don't need to be a technical expert to be an operator. However, having some expert tips and basic understanding can absolutely help make you be a better operator. The goal of this chapter is to give you information that will help you operate your brain better, so you and your brain work together, not against each other. I think it's a decent goal to want to be an expert in brain operations. It makes life so much easier.

Now that I've shown you the rainbow tutu covering my ass (my CYA strategy), let's get back to the good stuff.

You Are Not Your Thoughts

Thinking happens in your brain. Your brain is an organ in your body. Sure, those are pretty obvious statements, at first glance, but they have some pretty dramatic implications. (You have no idea how much restraint it took to not make a no-brainer joke.)

To start, you are not your brain. We tend to assume we are our brains because the brain is the primary place in our body where our awareness lives. But we can shift our awareness to other locations. We can step outside of our conscious brain. To repeat, the brain is an organ in your body, and it's arguably the most powerful tool we have. I like to think of the brain as a really, really powerful computer—and you are the user. I'm going to pepper that analogy in here pretty consistently.

If you are not your brain, you are also not your thoughts. You are the one thinking your thoughts. Test this out. Think about the sky. Visualize it. Imagine a blue sky with a few white clouds trailing across. Did you see it? Okay, now notice that you were thinking about the sky. You can do both. Think about the sky and notice that you are thinking about the sky. Yup, you are not your thoughts. There's huge power in this. You are not at the mercy of your thoughts. You are not a victim of your thoughts. You are not powerless. You can learn to manage your brain and manage your thoughts. You can choose which programs to run on your computer. It's a skill, similar to managing people. To be a good manager, you need to understand your employee (your brain), to know what motivates them and how you can help them to improve and be their best.

And like a problem employee, your brain can be bossy, but it doesn't have to be the boss of you. You have to actively decide to be the boss, take the reins and the responsibility to be a *good* boss. Educate yourself a bit. Practice. Review.

The Brain as a Distributed Network

I've just spent a few paragraphs talking about the brain as if it's a single entity. That's convenient, but not the whole story. The brain isn't an organ like the liver or kidney or gall bladder, with relatively specific functions. The brain is a collection of systems located in specific regions of the body. While there is still a lot of mystery around how and why this system works the way it does, we do know some useful things. For example, we can identify specific regions in the brain and the general functionality associated with those regions. Although, we cannot (yet) create a definitive map of what happens where. The brain functions similarly to a distributed network, a term used in IT (which stands for information technology—more computer stuff). Thinking and processing are interactions/communications between the regions. There are redundant pathways that protect key functionality, like an emergency backup system.

Let's take a moment to look at a few of these regions—five, to be exact—and what we know about them, starting with age before beauty. Literally.

Brain Stem

Let's start with the **brain stem**. This is the oldest part of the brain, where the primitive survival instincts live. Popular psychology has given us some great names for this region: Monkey mind, primitive brain, lizard brain, reptilian brain, and survival brain, to name a few. The brain stem's prime directive is to keep us alive by maintaining basic bodily functions, identifying threats, and responding to them. Oh, and we only need to stay alive long enough to pass on our genetic material. There is no thriving involved. The simplest rule for survival is to avoid pain. There's not a lot of processing power here—threats are not really evaluated, assessed for credibility, or prioritized; and there isn't any strategy as far as how to deal with the threats. The brain stem basically narrows things down to two options—fight or flight. Great in a pinch, yup, but not the brain region we want in charge of daily life.

Limbic System

Next up is the *limbic system*, which is often called the emotional brain. Again, there's no real consensus on what *exactly* makes up this system, but most agree it includes the hypothalamus, thalamus, amygdala, and hippocampus. The limbic system is where emotions, memory, and stimulation are primarily processed, which means it regulates endocrine function to produce the hormones that regulate your body and mind in response to emotional stimuli. The hypothalamus is in charge of releasing all these hormones. The amygdala rules the processing of fearful and anxious emotions. The hippocampus is associated with storing emotional memories. The thalamus coordinates motor and sensory signals, consciousness, sleep, mood, and alertness—it translates and transmits messages to the cerebral cortex. And that's enough detail on the limbic system. Wake up! You can research more if you want.

Cerebrum

The *cerebrum* is the largest part of the brain, usually considered the main part of the human brain. It's also called the control center. The cerebral cortex is the grey stuff on the outside of the cerebrum. It's the brains of the operation. (Sorry.) Intelligence, personality, planning, organization, language, perception, and processing all of that sensory information that comes in from the limbic system—those are the jobs of the cerebral cortex.

Prefrontal Cortex

The ***prefrontal cortex*** is the part of the cerebral cortex that covers the frontal lobe. In an article in the publication *The Neuropsychotherapist*, this region of the brain was "implicated in planning complex cognitive behavior, personality expression, decision making and moderating social behavior." I love that. "Implicated"! It sounds so conspiratorial, doesn't it? A better, but less fun explanation is that the prefrontal cortex is in charge of executive function, which is not at all the same function as what an executive does. Executive function involves differentiating between conflicting thoughts, determining degrees of behavior (bad, good, better, best), assessing future consequences, predictions and expectations, working toward goals, and assessing social implications. You know, grown-up stuff.

Hemispheres

Then there's the whole ***hemispheres*** thing. Right brain, left brain. The best explanation I've found (meaning the most relevant and easiest for me to incorporate here) is that the right brain identifies emotions and the left side interprets and makes decisions on what to do about them.

The Takeaway

While not by any means all-inclusive, these five regions of the brain are relevant for our purpose of understanding enough of how the brain works as a system of communication, interpretation, and processing. For me, the biggest takeaway is this: I don't need to take anything that comes from my brain at face value. Oh, and I need to step in and manage things if I want things to go my way. I need to control my mental agenda and the conversation.

Want a scenario of an unmanaged conversation? Here's one. When the brain stem and the amygdala dominate the conversation, you have survival instincts masquerading as thoughts amplified by fearful and anxious emotions. *Oh no! Warning, Will Robinson! Danger, danger! We're all gonna die.* Working together, the brain stem and amygdala lead us to believe the decision we're about to make is a matter of life and death, and they squirt stress hormones into the bloodstream, so we immediately want to jump into action. That's awesome, if we're being chased by a bear. It's probably not so awesome in response to an email from the IRS. We need the prefrontal cortex to assess the situation, remind us that the real IRS does not send emails, and help us decide NOT to click on the link or run to Wal-Mart and buy a bunch of $50 gift cards to pay off our back taxes.

Another way to think about how these different regions of the brain operate together is to use an analogy I've heard in twelve-step and self-improvement circles: The Committee. The Committee is a name for the different voices and thoughts that swirl around inside your head giving conflicting information or advice. When we don't manage The Committee, we usually end up stuck and afraid to take action, because we can't resolve the conflicting opinions. But if we recognize each committee member has their own motivation and their own agenda, we can begin to understand where these voices come from and decide how much attention to pay to them. Or we can decide to tell them, "Thank you, but be quiet now." That's a strategy we will definitely be using in Part 2.

We want to manage our brains, not the other way around. To be successful, we're going to need to know a few key concepts, aka management principles for the brain.

The Hierarchy

Perhaps you've heard of Abraham Maslow's hierarchy of needs? Well, our brain has a hierarchy of needs, too. It helps us to know the order of the brain's priorities because it's not an order that's aligned with our own goals—especially not our long-term goals.

Here's the brain's activation hierarchy:

#1 Survival! – The brain's number one job is to keep you around until tomorrow so you can perpetuate your genetic material. It's constantly scanning for danger.

#2 Pleasure – Once your safety has been ensured, the next job is to seek pleasure and reward you in the form of endorphins, dopamine, and serotonin.

#3 Efficiency – The brain uses a ton of energy to process information. Thinking is hard work. In order to save energy (calories), it looks for ways to become more efficient. One of the best ways to become efficient is to automate responses, decision-making, and routine actions, and to build neural pathways to make repetition easier and faster. Another way to say this is the brain seeks to "hardwire" rules and responses so you don't have to think so much, so you can go on "autopilot" and take a mental nap.

What's wrong with this picture? It sounds like it makes sense. Sounds can be deceiving. Let's peel off three layers, three things that are wrong with the practical application of letting your brain run on autopilot:

The need to put survival first is outdated. It evolved thousands of years ago when we faced threats to our survival on a daily basis. But in ordinary life today, that fear response actually holds us back. The brain can find danger in almost every situation, and no matter what the threat, the assessment is the same: *Noooo! You're gonna die.* The physical response is always fear, adrenalin, cortisol, and fight or flight (avoidance!)— whether you're being chased by a bear, opening a bill from the IRS, facing an uncomfortable emotion, or trying something new so you can grow.

The brain looks for immediate pleasure, not long-term well-being. Those brain chemicals are primarily short-term rewards, so seeking pleasure won't drive your brain to make a long-term investment in your career or health goals, for example. It will reward you for choosing a cookie, though! When you're making decisions in the moment, it's hard to resist immediate impulse gratification, even when doing so would be in our long-term best interest and get us what we really want.

The brain doesn't do automatic updates. As time goes on and we develop new goals, perspectives, and priorities, our automated responses can become out of sync with what we really want. We find our thoughts and behaviors in the moment don't seem to align with our goals and desires, and we can't seem to be successful at making the changes we want to make.

The Main Point

There's another impact of this hierarchy the brain uses. In order to be super-efficient and save energy, the brain loves to reduce things to binary thinking. Okay, maybe it doesn't actually *love* binary thinking, but when left to its own devices it will default to it.

Binary thinking is the process of reducing a situation down to only two variables, which are almost always mutually exclusive. Good or bad. Right or wrong. Yes or no. Stop or start. A or B. Black or white (Aha! No color!). All very clear-cut, with no overlap and no subtlety.

Binary thinking is great for analyzing danger, dealing with urgent issues, and driving us to action. It's a helpful starter tool for clarifying complex problems, creating sequences, and writing programming code.

But binary thinking definitely has a downside for us contemporary humans who spend most of our lives *not* in danger. Binary thinking is not only a result of survival thinking, it also triggers the related chemical reactions in our brains. It triggers a preoccupation with choosing the *right* answer because the only other option is the *wrong* answer. It triggers an adrenaline response. We know about the negative impacts of adrenaline and cortisol, the stress hormones.

In binary mode, we aren't always aware of some of its impacts. When we're running around on adrenaline, in flight or fight mode, we tend to see people as enemies. We become paranoid and isolated. Our reasoning becomes simplistic. We're easily exhausted. We don't have access to our creativity. And, in a social context, binary thinking, black-and-white thinking, is polarizing. I just realized that it would be more accurate to call it black-OR-white thinking. So, I will.

Black-or-white thinking also gets in the way of achieving our dreams. Your brain wouldn't have you think that's true. It's gonna try to convince you that it makes sense to narrow down your options, to break things down into incremental steps, making A-or-B choices along the way. Because, you know, if you have only two options, it's easier to decide, and it doesn't matter whether either option is awesome for you. You just have to decide.

But what really happens with black-or-white thinking is you start from a place of feeling at least slightly threatened. And, honestly, that doesn't feel great. That's stress. So, you set out to solve a problem, and you work through the problem by dismissing alternative solutions until you only have two options to decide between—the right one and the wrong one. The consequences of the decision get blown *waaaaay* out of proportion, because you've engaged a suspicious survival mechanism, one that perceives danger lurking behind each wrong choice. I call this *microdrama*—a state in which every little decision feels like it has momentous importance. It's overwhelming. It *is* overwhelm. It's often paralyzing. *Should I or shouldn't I? I can't decide...*

So, black-or-white thinking starts with stress and adds more. It "helps" you see enemies and risks where they might not even exist. And it literally shuts down your ability to see creative options. You cannot recognize alternatives. You cannot believe there might be more than one right answer... or a better or different approach. Black-or-white thinking is a lazy (energy-saving), primitive (survival-based) way to stay stuck on one side of an either/or equation, to live at one end of a polarized situation.

And then there's the logic argument... the one where your brain tells you black-or-white thinking is distilling things down to their essence, and if you remove your emotions from the equation, the right answer will become obvious. It's an interesting theory, but we have emotions for a reason. I'm going to open a loop here by saying that I will talk about emotions and their usefulness at the end of this chapter. For now, I'll say we need our emotions to achieve our dreams.

The bottom line is black-or-white thinking is a huge limiter of our potential. We don't need more *black* or *white*. We need options. We need color!

More Key Brain Concepts

Before we jump into Color Thinking, I want to introduce a few more concepts that will help us in Part 2.

And, yes, I'll still close that loop about emotions... just not yet.

Beliefs

Beliefs are like the roads our brain uses to navigate as we travel along on our lives. We create beliefs when we have enough information to detect a pattern. It's one way our brains can be efficient. There's a lot of incoming information to sort through, and the brain needs to know what to do with it. Even deciding to ignore information is a decision that takes energy.

In order to save on processing time and energy, the brain builds some automation, in the form of beliefs, so we don't have to re-examine and re-evaluate every time we encounter a similar situation—we can just process based on previous conclusions. The brain wants to keep the off-roading to a minimum and keep to the well-traveled roads. Some of these roads are so well-traveled they've become ruts.

The brain, again being both smart and lazy, doesn't always come up with its own roads. Sometimes, it takes over other people's beliefs—like squatter's rights—because it trusts them. That's how you end up finding some of your mom's old beliefs in your closet, for example. You might have outgrown your mom's beliefs, but chances are they're still hiding in your brain's closet, behind and underneath a whole pile of other outdated and ill-fitting beliefs., because it's a lot of work to clean out a closet. You have to set aside the time to work through the piles, evaluate the fit, throw stuff out, take stuff to the shop for tailoring, and go shopping for new beliefs. It doesn't happen unless you make it happen. So, you keep driving down those rutty roads wearing your mom's old beliefs. Wow, I do like to mix my metaphors, don't I?

Let me throw in this little tidbit: A belief is a thought we have thought so many times that we believe it. Beliefs don't have to be true. We just think they're true. Or, even more accurately, we just *assume* they're true because we haven't checked the evidence lately. Thoughts can only be believed if they're repeated.

The point is, we run our lives most of the time on autopilot. We drive around in our Black-or-White-Thinking-mobile (aka BWT), following the ruts of our outdated beliefs. These ruts are so ingrained we don't even know they're there. No wonder we keep ending up in the same place!

There are two more concepts I'd like to introduce about beliefs, to help you recognize them when you see them on the road later on. These two concepts are the seatbelts that keep our butts firmly in place in our BWTs.

The first is **confirmation bias**, which refers to the way your brain tends to search for, remember, and even interpret information that supports your preexisting thoughts and beliefs (heavy emphasis on the *interpret* part.) We see things through the lens of what we already think and believe and use that as evidence to reinforce our beliefs. Definitely a BWT seatbelt, right?

The second concept is **cognitive dissonance**, which is that uncomfortable feeling you have when you're in the midst of having conflicting thoughts and beliefs. It's that state of tension between your old thoughts and beliefs and the new ones you're trying to introduce. It's like driving around in your BWT when the wheels are out of alignment—a very bumpy and uncomfortable ride. It's often enough to make us give up and go back to the old beliefs, just because it's a smoother ride, even if our old beliefs won't take us where we want to go.

Emotions

Here I am, closing the emotions loop. Did it make you a little uncomfortable that I overtly opened a loop and then left it hanging open for so long? That's another thing to know about our brains: They really don't like leaving things unresolved. They will work very hard to try to close that loop, sometimes even making stuff up to close it.

My brain *really* hates an open loop. I used to drive my mother crazy. She would be telling me a story and maybe mumble a little bit. If I didn't catch exactly what she'd said, an alarm would go off in my brain (*Whoop whoop whoop! Open loop! Unresolved aural fragment!*) and, in self-defense, I would feel forced to ask her to repeat herself. But she had only been casually talking and couldn't remember the exact words she'd used, so she couldn't repeat the exact phrase. She'd resort to explaining what she meant, which did nothing to help me close that aural loop. For many years, in those situations, I'd be an asshole and tell her explaining didn't help and I needed to figure out exactly what she'd said. I finally realized those were a nice opportunity to manage my brain. I could intentionally make something up that sounded similar to what she'd said and tell my brain it could relax because the loop had been closed. It helped that some of the things I made up were highly entertaining.

There were a few emotions in that story. Did you notice them? What exactly are emotions? They're intense sensations usually linked to thoughts about one's situation or circumstances. These sensations are feelings in the body—physical responses to chemical messages from the brain.

I say emotions are *usually* linked to thoughts about situations because there are exceptions. One exception is in the case of an empath, someone who feels the emotions associated with someone else's thoughts. Another exception is emotions tied to hormonal rhythms, which often can't be directly linked to specific thoughts. And there's the exception of a chemical imbalance in the neurotransmitters of the brain. But those are the exceptions. I'm going to focus here on the general rule.

The general rule is our emotions are part of a chain reaction. There is a situation. The brain processes the information about it, then delivers a thought and a chemical message to create an emotion (or multiple emotions). Emotions motivate us to *do* something—to take action, to avoid, to show up a certain way, to think more thoughts, etc. The actions we take affect our situation, the next link in the chain.

Many, many coaches make a living helping people understand this process—this model for human behavior—and how to intervene to make it work to create a better life. It's an admirable vocation, and a great place to start. But it's not the be-all and end-all process, however, and figuring out a better way was a big part of the reason I was finally able to stop chasing life-coaching certifications. I knew there had to be more to the story.

Yes, emotions are powerful motivators. We crave certain emotions and will do just about anything to get more of them. We fear other emotions and will go to great lengths to avoid feeling them. In fact, the amount of time we spend avoiding those emotions is a huge waste of time and energy. Take humiliation, for example. We avoid it like the plague. But, you know, it isn't the plague. You can die from the plague. You can't die from humiliation. Your face might turn red. Your pulse might quicken. You might feel nauseous. But you won't die. The feeling passes pretty quickly, unless we keep reminding ourselves of the source of our humiliation, worrying the event like a dog licking a sore paw. When we understand that we won't die from humiliation, that it will pass, we can be much more realistic in our assessments of risks and consequences. We might be willing to take bigger risks along the way toward our dreams and goals.

Understanding how emotions motivate us helps us take control of the emotion chain reaction. But we don't need to stop there. Emotions have several additional functions.

Emotions are indicators of our hidden beliefs. Let's use jealousy as an example. Jealousy is an indicator that you want something, but you believe you can't have it. Jealousy unlocks a secret, outdated belief that doesn't serve you. Instead of falling into the rut of that automatic belief, you could change what you want. Or change what you believe about yourself.

Let's talk about shame. Shame tells you that you've bought into somebody else's belief system about who you should be and how you should live your life—and you aren't living up to it. The secret is to figure out who YOU want to be.

These are just two examples of how emotions can indicate hidden beliefs. There are many more.

Emotions are a form of intelligence. We can feel emotions before we know why we feel them, before the brain has finished processing the logic and delivering a thought. Emotions are indicators of our intuition, messages that come from our gut. If we are empathic—and I believe most of us are— we can use emotions to learn to access the collective wisdom that lives outside our own brain.

Finally, emotions are reactions to real or imagined situations—our brain doesn't know the difference. This bit is important. In *The Rainbow Onion* work, we use the power of our imaginations to intentionally create emotions that help us create the outcomes we desire.

To sum up:

- You are not your brain, and you are not your thoughts.
- Even neuroscientists can't agree on everything.
- Your brain is a complex conglomeration of processes.
- Your brain is doing its best to protect you but uses some outdated methods.
- Your brain needs to be supervised, and you're the one for the job.
- Some key concepts can help you be a better brain manager.
- Emotions are included in your manager's toolbox.

The bottom line: all is not lost. We can absolutely update our beliefs, and we can get out of our BWT vehicle. We just need to add some Color Thinking! It can be like that magical moment when Dorothy wakes up in Oz and discovers a life in ultra-high-definition Technicolor.

By the way, all this stuff I just spent pages and pages describing? It's not saying something is broken or wrong or malicious inside your head. It's to explain that your brain is working as designed, but it's been working unsupervised. If you want to get more out of your brain, you're gonna have to step into that management role. Color Thinking is your new brain management tool.

Color Thinking Story – Amara

Once upon a time, I was working with a client, Amara, who just happened to be one of my most favorite humans. She was at a big turning point. She was making all the changes she needed to make to create the life of her dreams—and it was working. She was doing it.

But Amara had a long history of black-or-white thinking, and when she encountered a challenge or two, she had a tendency to fall back into it without being aware she was doing it. She would get stuck. She would have a hard time seeing options and making decisions. She would say she felt like she was in survival mode—and she was because her black-or-white thinking triggered the adrenaline response, complete with fear and polarization.

Amara consistently tried to narrow her options until she had only two, so she could distinguish the *right* option from the *wrong* option. Then she became paralyzed, afraid she would pick the wrong one.

We tried adding shades of grey between the black and white options, but that didn't really work. Amara would take the grey options and move them closer and closer to one end or the other until she had only two options left again. I could hear how trapped she felt. I could hear the frustration and discouragement in her tone of voice. I needed to come up with another way for her to look at things.

One day, I asked Amara what her favorite color was, and she said, "Orange!" The way she said it was so different from how she'd been talking that I immediately knew we were on to something. She sounded excited and happy and her voice suddenly had energy. *Okay*, I thought, *we can work with this!*

"So," I asked Amara, "what is an orange idea here? What is an orange option?"

She immediately came up with a new option. And then another. And another. She had translated my question to mean "what is an option you would love?" and then tapped into her creativity to be able to brainstorm without judging, without seeking to find the one right answer. She was no longer fearful. In fact, she was having fun.

Together we worked with orange thinking a lot. Initially, orange thinking opened up the door of noticing a third option (not black or white)—which, by the way, is the doorway to genius. But orange thinking continued to grow. It developed layers. We started to layer in the different meanings of the color orange—the universal, cultural, personal, and spiritual meanings. It was new. It was fun. And Amara's transformation became truly meteoric.

Orange is hard to miss. It's explosive and bright. It sticks out. It's enthusiastic, warm, creative, and fun. It is used to represent freedom and caution. The infused orange can represent following your bliss, but the saturated orange, the other end of the orange spectrum, represents a need to heal the timeline, to recover from shock or trauma.

For Amara, the orange thinking work was to rewrite her past, dump the limiting beliefs, write her new story, and actively seek evidence that supported her new, unlimited beliefs.

My friend Rob says we don't need to see more shades of grey between black and white; we need to see the rainbow of options between them. That's it exactly!

And that's the story of how Color Thinking was born.

Color Thinking Exercise – Build Your Own Color Vocabulary (2)

For this exercise, you'll continue to build your color lingo, adding another two columns to your worksheet—Personal and Emotional:

Personal – In this column, list meanings that come from your own personal life experiences.

Emotional – List emotions you associate with each color. What emotions does this color evoke in you? Emotions can be anywhere on the spectrum.

As you fill in these columns, remember to look at the color and the name of the color, because seeing the color helps invoke your responses.

***

This chapter is packed with a lot of information about the brain, how and why it functions the way it does, and how beliefs are formed. We also covered a few key concepts, such as how black-or-white thinking is NOT in your long-term best interest, confirmation bias, cognitive dissonance, open loops, and… emotions. Emotions are indicators of what you are thinking. You won't die from an emotion. That's pretty helpful to know for when you start telling your brain it isn't the boss of you.

When you've finished adding more to your color vocabulary, we'll move on to put color and thinking together!

CHAPTER 3

PUT THEM TOGETHER, COLOR THINKING

"Salagadoola mechicka boola

Bibbidi-bobbidi-boo

Put them together and what have you got?

Bibbidi-bobbidi-boo

Salagadoola mechicka boola

Bibbidi-bobbidi-boo

It'll do magic, believe it or not

Bibbidi-bobbidi-boo."

—Cinderella's Fairy Godmother, *Cinderella*

It might sound like nonsense to put disparate things together. Like sounds, or like strawberries and hot sauce. Or like color and thinking. But sometimes those combinations are magical!

In the last chapter, in Amara's Color Thinking Story, I told you how Color Thinking was born. In this chapter, I'll explain a bit about that combination and why it works. Then, in Part 2, to really help you understand Color Thinking, we'll walk through in detail how to do it.

To review, if we want to evolve to the next version of ourselves, we're going to have a much easier time if we start proactively taking on the management position with our brains. To do that, we have to break out of the ruts we've been using to navigate. We have to go off-roading on purpose.

To go off-road, we have to interrupt the patterns we're stuck in now. What are those patterns? We went pretty deep into black-or-white thinking in the last chapter, but there are also other patterns that can keep us stuck.

Here are a few examples:

- We might be consistently stuck trying to reconcile our head and our heart, ping-ponging back and forth. I call that dithering.
- We might be so firmly entrenched in the detail we can't see the big picture, and we never seem to make progress. Or vice versa: Stuck in the big picture, can't find the details, and don't make progress.
- We might have a cycle of self-sabotage.
- We might live in an inner world of self-doubt, guilt, shame, self-loathing, or some other kind of negative self-judgment.
- We might have a gigantic victim mythology going on, spending all our time waiting for a fairy godfather or princess charming to come along and rescue us.
- We might have an unpublished rulebook for other people, full of all the conditions that need to be met for us to love them or accept them or be happy.
- We could be trapped in a pessimistic half-empty glass full o' fear, too paralyzed to take the tiniest risk.

- We might be convinced we're trapped in a confined space, with no options at all, not even black or white.

There's no way I'd be able to list all of the potential patterns that could be running our lives because the variations are pretty much infinite. No matter what the details of the ruts are, the cause is the same: We're running our lives on outdated software. We have outdated beliefs that do not serve us. They keep us stuck. We're unable to progress, to change, to grow into the versions of ourselves we want to become.

We have to turn the autopilot off and take hold of the controls ourselves. We have to learn to manage our own brains. We have to choose new beliefs and create enough support that we can go out and find the evidence we need to believe them. We need to bring in tools to overcome confirmation bias and cognitive dissonance. There are many ways to do thought work.

Color Thinking is a new type of thought work. I happen to love it. Let me tell you why. This is a list of why I love Color Thinking, but it's also the list of why Color Thinking works.

It's fun – I love color. It helps me access the creative parts of my brain to solve whatever problem I'm working on. It feels playful.

It's sensory – Color Thinking is not just an intellectual exercise. The name tells you that, right? We blend a visual language with a thinking language to create new forms of expression, to see things in a new way.

It's new – Because it's new, it doesn't come with a lot of baggage. You can't say, "I tried that before and it didn't work." Well, you could say that, but it wouldn't be true. Color Thinking has that new-idea smell.

It's quick – It's the stuff of breakthroughs. Some types of thought work are tedious—Color Thinking isn't. It doesn't take years and years to do. There can be rapid—even instantaneous — shifts in perspective.

It's reusable – Color Thinking is a set of skills. You can do it once, on one layer, and get good at it, because it's mostly using your color language, and it's certainly your brain and your life. So you become your own expert. And you can do it again on the next layers!

It's the opposite of polarizing – I guess that means it's unifying. It's certainly cohesive. You find and see the patterns, similarities, and commonalities, in you and in other people. Color Thinking does not need any enemies to work.

It's diverse – Why do we love a rainbow or a garden with lots of different colors of types of flowers, or the Northern Lights? Variety. Choices. Adventure. Depth. Abundant opportunities.

It's intentional – In Color Thinking, we get to choose what we want to think, believe, and do. We get to pick the outcome we want to construct.

It doesn't conflict with other tools. There's no incompatibility with other types of thought work, with different coaching models, spiritual practices, belief systems, or tools. Color thinking doesn't require you to pick a new religion. You can use affirmations and crystals and chakra colors. You can use prayer and candles. Or not. You can use Color Thinking with whatever else works for you. In fact, Color Thinking pairs pretty well with almost anything—except, of course, those outdated beliefs that are holding you back. It does conflict with those buggers.

It's universal but specific – Color Thinking is a layer cake built out of universal, cultural, and other contextual understandings. The cake, however, is in the shape of your own life. It applies specifically to you and whatever is going on in your life right now. It's practical.

It's efficient – Color Thinking requires us to spend just enough time in the past to be able to see what the problem is—to find out exactly what the outdated belief is—but we don't need to stay any longer than that. We don't keep visiting and reliving the old shit and thus putting it back into our short-term memory. We only need to recognize the old stuff so we can squish it with our pointy-toed boots when it pops up!

Color Thinking works, as you'll see in the stories about it. It's transformational. It's a tool for making dramatic change for good.

Now that I've whetted your appetite, here is my definition of Color Thinking, expressed in two parts:

Color Thinking is a powerful tool to use in thought work. It uses the language of color to create new patterns of thinking to support you on your journey to become who you want to be.

Color Thinking is also a powerful tool for reconciliation. You start by reconciling your beliefs with who you want to be, and healing the differences.

I can't tell you how many iterations I had to go through to come up with that definition! I like it. It might continue to morph a bit between now and the time this goes to print.

The Rainbow Onion

The Rainbow Onion is what I call the process, the methodology, the program for applying Color Thinking—right now, right where you are, at whatever layer you're excavating.

The Rainbow Onion process works by taking you from your current story through transformational pattern interruption, intentional redirection, the construction of a new framework, and with the necessary support. Doesn't that sound technical? Or maybe mysterious. Well, in the next section of the book, Part 2, it will all become crystal clear as we will walk through the detailed steps of *The Rainbow Onion* process. More will be revealed, as they say.

For now, let me tell you a short pink story, then you can finish up your color vocabulary worksheet and we'll move on to the guts of it all.

Color Thinking Story – Jordan

Our story starts with Jordan. Jordan felt like shit. He was stuck in a black-or-white pattern, but he didn't see it. He was so entrenched in his old patterns that he absolutely believed they were true.

His pattern applied whenever he thought he was excluded or left out—when he wasn't invited to something, when he wasn't asked to do a task at work, when he wasn't offered the same opportunity someone else was.

When he felt excluded by someone, he KNEW it was either because he sucked or because they didn't care about him. No other possibility. He even applied it to when he thought someone SHOULD include him, as if they should be able to read his mind.

Can you imagine how much that always hurt? Believing those were the only possible reasons behind every real or imagined slight?

We knew where his pattern came from: his deep-seated fears of abandonment and rejection because his parents had abandoned him. But Jordan also had lots of experiences where people had chosen him and were loyal and loved him very much. But that confirmation bias thing kept him from being able to see the positive experiences as evidence that perhaps his automatic pattern was wrong. Knowing where his beliefs came from was not enough to send them packing.

We used Color Thinking to understand which color's saturated shadow side (the negative aspects) resonated most strongly with where he was, and which infused side (the positive aspects) matched the direction he most wanted to move toward.

He chose pink.

The saturated shadow side of pink shows up when we're exceptionally hard on ourselves, judgmental of others, living in the critical, and surrounded by negativity. We need pink thinking when we notice we're feeling shame, blame, guilt, hurt, self-pity, and defensiveness about ourselves, or anger, resentment, and judgment toward others. That's definitely where Jordan was living.

The infused side of pink is a gentle color, full of light and feminine mother energy. Pink brings unconditional love, self-acceptance, caring, compassion, open-mindedness, and acceptance of others. It allows us to be vulnerable. That's where Jordan wanted to be.

Once we agreed pink thinking was the thing for Jordan, he needed to look at his thinking. But he was so stuck in it he couldn't see it, right? So, we had to ask some pink questions (we will get into color questions soon), which went something like this:

- What can I think and believe that will make me feel less critical of myself (or someone else)?
- What thoughts would be more accepting and compassionate?
- How can I look at this situation in a way that is more supportive and less judgmental?
- What would unconditional love do in this situation?
- How can I be that love?
- What do I already believe that's in line with pink?

Those questions allowed Jordan to step outside his own thought patterns and see maybe, just maybe, some of the things people did that he'd interpreted as exclusion had absolutely nothing to do with him. People might be choosing based on their own reasons. And that opened up a crack just wide enough that he could begin to see some other possible explanations and find new evidence and new ways to interpret the evidence. It was possible people could care about him AND want to do things for their own motivations.

Of course, there's more to Jordan's story – like how he handled it when cognitive dissonance kicked in, when the old patterns showed up, and how he kicked them out. That's a story for Part 2.

Color Thinking Exercise — Finish Your Color Vocabulary

For this chapter, you'll finish your personal color vocabulary (PCV) by adding the final two columns to your worksheet. Remember to look at both the color and the name of the color, because seeing the color helps invoke your responses.

The two column titles to add are Spiritual and Memories.

Spiritual – What are some spiritual meanings or associations you have with this color?

Memories – Building on the personal and emotional, list any key words that will remind you of stories, events, insights, etc.—to help you easily access your understanding of that color and what it says to you.

And voila! You're done with your personal color vocabulary, right? Oh, not really. You'll continue to discover and remember more personal meanings for color. You'll build your language. You can come back and update your PCV (because we need some acronyms here!). Or you can make up another way to keep a record.

It will be fun to watch how your understanding of your color language deepens over time. It's also quite handy to have it written down, so you can refer to it when you want it. I can't tell you how often I use mine!

***

Well, Part 1 is now a wrap. We've covered color as a language. We've covered thinking. And we've put them together to make this magical new thing called **Color Thinking**.

Let's move on to the guts—*The Rainbow Onion* process—and how to use it.

PART 2

THE RAINBOW ONION PROCESS

"That's how good you don't even know you are!"

—Jonathan Groff

This section, Part 2, walks you through *The Rainbow Onion* process—how you "do" Color Thinking—by working on your own stuff in your own life, because that's the best and fastest way to really learn it. I won't just give you general instructions. I'll walk you through how to do your own process. You'll learn by doing.

Before we start, you're going to need to figure out what you want to work on. Of course, the first question most everyone asks is "How do I pick the thing?" My favorite answer is "What do you want to work on?" *That* is usually the thing—whatever is top of your mind. But if you don't have a clear answer, then play with these questions:

- What's the one emotion you crave? If you could change one thing to be able to feel more of that emotion, what would you change?

- What's the story/reason/excuse you hear yourself telling too much?

- What's the one emotion (or cluster of related emotions) you wish you didn't feel so frequently?
- What's the one thing that, if you dealt with it and made it easier, would clear away most of the garbage that gets in your way?
- Is there something you think everyone else has mastered, but you haven't—and you can't figure out why?

If something to work on jumps out from those questions, awesome. Pick that as your thing. If you still got nothing, pick one thing that bugs you. Anything. Or put some things on the wall and throw a dart! It almost doesn't matter what you choose, because it will work itself out. You'll see what you need to see. I don't believe there are any coincidences, so whatever you pick will be what you need to pick.

There's this saying that makes its way around the coaching world: *How you do one thing is how you do everything*. While I don't think it is 100% accurate, it definitely has some truth. You have patterns, and they will emerge if we look deep enough at any one thing.

If you're worrying too much about picking THE RIGHT THING, you've just given yourself a great example of black-or white-thinking! There isn't any one right thing. There are layers.

Color Thinking Exercise – Pick Your Thing

Just pick it. That's Your Thing. This is the technical term for what you're gonna work on during *The Rainbow Onion* process: Your Thing.

If you're using your own journal for this process, make sure you write down what Your Thing is. If you want to download that printable workbook, it's still available to you as bonus content (it wasn't an offer that expired in

Part 1!). Just go to **therainbowonion.com/bonus** and sign up. You'll get the password to the site, and you'll be able to download the workbook and other bonus content.

Here's What's in Store for You

You'll spend a lot of time doing thought work—the thinking part of Color Thinking. In fact, Chapters 4 through 6 are mostly focused on thought work. To keep us connected to the color aspect of Color Thinking, I'll continue to bring in color stories. As soon as we get to Chapter 7, you'll be bringing in your own personal color to the process.

Here are the chapters in Part 2:

Chapter 4 – Step 1: Tell Your Story – Your story is your version of history. It probably feels very true to you. It doesn't have to be that way. You can rewrite it. But first, you're gonna have to tell it one more time— one last time—in detail.

Chapter 5 – Step 2: Analyze Your Story – Now you're going to look at your story—without judging—so you can see what your story is creating in your life. Where are those outdated beliefs showing up, and how are they holding you back?

Chapter 6 – Step 3: Find the Gem – You'll boil the story down to its essence. What are you making this whole thing mean about you?

Chapter 7 – Step 4: Prescribe Your Color – You'll diagnose yourself and find the color you need—the one with the saturated, shadow attributes that describe where you are now and the infused, bright attributes you crave.

Chapter 8 – Step 5: Interrupt with Colorful Questions – You'll interrupt your pattern and change the frame of reference with powerful questions based on the color you've chosen.

Chapter 9 – Step 6: Redirect – You'll begin to redirect your pattern by deciding and declaring your goal, and then deciding what you need to believe in order to achieve it. Wait, what? Read on...

Chapter 10 – Step 7: Build the Best Belief for You – This is where we dig into your old beliefs and craft your new ones. It's like you get to be part of the Maker Movement!

Chapter 11 – Step 8: Plan the Magic in Color – This is where you set up all the support you'll need to be able to stay on your redirected path... and there are lots of support options. You'll create your own personalized support system. This work does NOT need to be scary or miserable or even particularly hard. It might even be fun and feel wonderful. It might be magical. It's certainly colorful!

Chapter 12 – What to Expect – Of course there will be some surprises as you do *The Rainbow Onion* process. Maybe a setback or two, a temptation or motivation challenge along the way. If you know what to expect, you can plan for it. (Major spoiler alert: Having a plan is the best way to handle a challenge!)

Okay, so that's what's coming up. You can see that there are many layers to this process. I suggest you take your time and savor the journey. Let's start with your story...

CHAPTER 4

STEP 1: TELL YOUR STORY

"If you will let your dominant intention be to revise and improve the content of the story you tell every day of your life, it is our absolute promise to you that your life will become that ever-improving story."

—Abraham-Hicks

Storytelling is an art form that has been around since people started communicating with each other. It's a part of the human experience. I'm not sure humans are the only storytellers. My cat sure has a lot to say when he comes in from outside, and I'm convinced he's telling me the story of his recent escapades. He's pretty dramatic, too.

Stories were used way before writing ever became a thing. Stories are narratives that have many uses: To teach, to pass along moral values, to share cultural traditions, and to track history, to name just a few. Stories are entertaining, and a good story is really effective.

Here's a fun thing about stories: they can be full of contradictions. They can be historically inaccurate, factually challenged, maybe even pure fantasy—and yet they can still tell us something about truth. Think about myths and fables and legends as examples of this.

What about our personal stories? Same thing.

When we put a narrative together of our own personal history, that's a story. We (and our brains) tell stories to explain how and why things have happened in our lives. We create stories to fill our need for explanations. We interpret events, choices, thoughts, and other mysterious things in a way that makes sense to us. We connect things into a cohesive narrative, so we can make sense of it all.

Sometimes we embellish a little, to put ourselves in a better light or to explain the inexplicable. That's not lying—that's how the brain works.

And then we tell that story. To others. To ourselves. We repeat it. The more we repeat it, the more embedded it becomes. The more we believe it. Our beliefs become the structure of the story. We become our story.

That would be awesome, if we updated our stories to keep up with our personal growth and evolution. It would be awesome if our stories were full of potential and optimism and motivation—you know, like the stories we told when we were kids, where we're stars and superheroes. But as we grow up, our stories and our roles in them tend to change and get stuck. Maybe we have a story that we're a victim, or different, or ashamed or guilty, or have flaws we need to hide.

You know what? We can update our stories. We just have to take the time to do it. We have to make the time to do it. You can completely rewrite your history into a more honest, more hopeful, more empathetic, more insightful and more supportive way. You do not need to be limited by your story. Your updated story can become one of the most powerful things in your toolbox.

When you rewrite your story, you can help heal your past wounds. You heal your personal timeline. I am not talking about historical negationism like the denial of the Holocaust. I'm talking about legitimate historical revisionism—adding in new information and evidence, reinterpreting and refining the narrative based on insights and learnings—to create a more accurate history.

Before we can dig into the details of our narrative to find the flaws, limitations and outdated evidence, we need to know those details. One last time, tell your old story. Throw in all the juicy, gory details. Get it out of your system. Write it all down, knowing that this is the last time you will tell this story as your true and current story.

When you change your story, you change your understanding of the past, which gives you the opportunity to create a new future.

And, by the way, you are not just your story. You might think you are, but you are so much more. We'll clean up the story part anyway because it's the easiest layer to start working on.

Color Thinking Story – Jenna

Here's how Jenna told her story:

Every time something good happens, I'm waiting for the other shoe to drop. Because if something good happens, something equally bad or even worse happens. It's been that way my whole life. Ever since I was a child. Don't get too happy or feel too settled, because we will have to move, or I'll break my arm or we'll lose all our money or someone will die. That's what happened. And it's continued throughout my adult life.

Want proof?

I got a good job, and my husband was diagnosed with cancer a couple of months later. I finished getting my master's degree, and right afterward we had something major happen with each of our cars.

I can go on and on. I have so many examples. I could give you so much proof. I'm cursed. Anything good is too good to be true. I'm afraid of getting a new job because someone will probably have to die. I'm terrified of hoping for good things to happen, because I know that means something bad will happen. I'm pretty much doomed to stay exactly where I am."

The essence of her story (Jenna's gem) is *I am cursed.*

If you could hear the tone of Jenna's voice when telling her story, you would know just how committed she is to this being the story— "the truth"—of her life. For Jenna, this zero-sum game is the explanation of how life works for her. Not for everyone, just for her. Not for her sister—who, according to Jenna, is somehow mysteriously blessed with wonderful things: A healthy family, a nice home, a comfortable lifestyle, and a satisfying career. Jenna doesn't resent the fact that her sister has wonderful things. She wants her sister to be happy and healthy and secure. But Jenna is jealous because she doesn't believe those things are possible for her.

Her conviction is almost unshakeable. She truly sees no other explanation. She's convinced there's a karmic connection between getting a master's degree and the car breaking down on the freeway. Talk about confirmation bias, right?

I could see a couple of other ways to look at things, different spins on interpreting the evidence. First, we aren't just gifted with master's degrees out of the goodness of the Universe's heart. We have to work for it. I know—I have a couple. And I've had a car break down on the freeway before. Sometimes it happened because I had an older car, or I had let the maintenance slip. Sometimes machines just break down.

Maybe landing a good job is awesome to do before your husband needs medical benefits. What if it meant you were super lucky, not cursed?

I might not be any more correct in my alternate interpretations than Jenna is—but my point is there are other ways to look at things that might be more helpful. There is definitely an opportunity for Jenna to revise her particular history. And she's going to add color to it, too, so stay tuned!

Color Thinking Exercise – Tell Your Story about Your Thing

You have lots of stories. You don't need them all for this step. Your story for this exercise doesn't need to be your life story or a complete autobiography. In the last chapter, you picked Your Thing to work on. For now, tell the part of your life story that has to do with Your Thing.

Tell your story with as much detail as you can, because the details will be helpful in the next step. The devil is in the details, right? Don't edit. Don't judge. Don't try to correct your story along the way. Don't worry about how you look—this is only for you!

Remember that you can go get the workbook at **therainbowonion.com/bonus**, and if you decide to do that later, you can always come back here to the book to get the link.

***

Congrats! You've taken the first step—and it's a big one—toward changing your story to something better. The next step will be to put on your lab coat.

CHAPTER 5

STEP 2: ANALYZE YOUR STORY

"I wish we could stop the little lies. I don't mean that one has to be brutally frank. I don't believe that we should be brutal about anything, however, it is wonderfully liberating, to be honest. One does not have to tell all that one knows, but we should be careful what we say is the truth."

—Maya Angelou

Now that you've told your story, it's time to take a good hard look at it. It's time to analyze your story. I'm going to ask you to do something that might be a bit difficult. Don't judge. Don't try to figure out who the characters are (Who is the villain? Who is the hero?). Don't try to place blame. If you're accustomed to beating yourself up for everything you do wrong, this is going to be a BIG challenge for you. Like Maya says in the quote above, you don't have to be brutal about it —just be wonderfully and liberatingly honest.

Here's a trick to make it easier: Decide you're going into this as a research scientist, and then play the part and stick with it. You work in a lab (your life), and your story is an experiment you're analyzing.

As a research scientist, you wear a lab coat and goggles, and sometimes you even need to wear gloves. These protect you from messy and dangerous goo. They also keep you safely distanced from the experiment.

Your job is to observe the experiment, gather data, and analyze it. Your job requires you to be objective, which means you need to leave your preconceived ideas and assumptions at the door and walk into the lab with an open mind and open eyes. You aren't here to make the data fit a theory. In fact, you shouldn't even start out with a theory!

If it's too big a stretch to think of yourself as a research scientist, you can try being a detective. A detective has more flexibility with their outfit, but they also observe situations and gather data.

In either case, you'll read through your story, make observations, and mark it up. Your responses shouldn't be any more judgmental than observations like "Huh, that's interesting" or "Well, that's curious. I wonder why I chose to tell the story like that."

You need to step outside of the story and look at it AS A STORY, not as fact, not as a list of your failures or successes. Seriously, the hardest part of looking at your story will probably be stepping away from judgment—but that's also the most valuable part. When you can look at your story about Your Thing objectively, you can begin to see the places where it could fall apart, where it's being held together by duct tape and baling wire.

What's Your Analysis?

Here are some questions to help you analyze your story and assess its impacts. Feel free to add questions of your own, as long as they're helpful!

- So what is going on with my story?

- What kind of story is this? Is it a fable? A myth? A mystery? A parable? Or something else?
- What's the purpose of my story? What is it trying to explain?
- When did I start telling myself this story? Why?
- Who is telling the story? Is it me? Do I hear other voices in the narrative?
- Who are the main characters?
- What is my role?
- What assumptions did I make?
- Are there any interesting word choices?
- Are there any questionable elements—things that are stated as facts, but are really assumptions? Are there misinterpretations of facts?
- Do I notice a confirmation bias?
- Is there missing information?
- Are there any obvious opportunities for the "evidence" to be reinterpreted?
- What might need to be re-examined? What parts of this story might no longer be true?

Take a Breather

Let's take a break for a minute to introduce some color, because you've been thinking a lot. Let's do some color breathing. Pale pink is always a good choice for this, because—as you've seen from Jordan's story—pink brings in unconditional love, self-acceptance, caring, compassion, and open-mindedness. Pink allows us to be vulnerable. If pink doesn't calm you, pick a color that does.

Now visualize the color in your mind's eye as you breathe in for a count of four, hold for four, breathe out for four, and hold for four again. Repeat this four times.

Put this exercise in your pocket and carry it with you, because you can do it anytime you feel overwhelmed.

What's the Impact?

Next you're going to look at the impact of your story, at how you've been using it. Since you need to continue to be honest, loving, and gentle with yourself, that pink breathing will have set you up wonderfully. You'll be digging into the "so what?" of your story by answering some more questions.

- Have I been using this story for myself or against myself?
- What do I make this story mean? About me, about others, about life, etc.?
- Up to this point, what thoughts have I repeatedly had about my story?
- What emotions come up *in* my story *about* my story?
- How has this story influenced my actions?
- Do I notice any behavioral patterns?
- Looking at this story with fresh eyes, what thoughts do I have about it right now?
- And how do I feel about my story now?
- How might this story have served me in the past?
- Is this story serving me today?

The Results of Your Research

Look, this is a big deal. You and your story have probably been pretty much interchangeable up to this point. It's very likely you don't even know it's a story—it just seems like your true autobiography. But it isn't. Until you take control of your story and write it the way you want, YOUR STORY OWNS YOU. Your story could be full of outdated beliefs and you don't even recognize them, because you're running on autopilot.

So how do you even know if you're running on autopilot?

Well, your body can tell you when your stories are running you. You have an early warning system. Your body tells you by giving you indicator emotions such as guilt, shame, or jealousy. You can feel stress, tension, and aches. Warnings show up in your body language, like in an involuntary sigh. Your body has muscle memory—which can be fantastic if you use it to improve your tennis swing or learn a dance step. But it's not awesome when muscle memory is tied to the negative impacts of a story and shows up in your posture, breathing, and your emotions (which are feelings in your body, remember?)

I had one client who went through a very difficult time for several months. She would go running for stress relief. Several times a week she would run on the same trail while thinking about the stress and emotions she was releasing. The running worked. But a year or so later, she noticed that when she ran that trail those same thoughts and emotions would come back, even though her situation was completely different by then. What the...? As she ran that trail, she repeated her story in her muscle memory. Even though her intention was relief, the original emotions she'd felt when running that trail in the past were still part of the story, and her body remembered. The story and the emotions were part of her muscle memory. That was an indication that she was running (literally) on autopilot. All she had to do to take control was switch things up—pick a different running route—and she was no longer on autopilot. It wasn't a difficult solution, but she'd needed to be able to notice the impact so she could change up the story.

Another way to know if you're running on autopilot is to look objectively at your story, like you just did in this chapter, and notice what doesn't fit anymore. If your story isn't working for you, take it off autopilot. STOP TELLING IT!

Consider this: If you could change anything about your story, what would you change? What WILL you change?

Color Thinking Story – Judy

In Judy's story, she also uses orange, but differently than how it was used in Amara's story, because Color Thinking is a personal and richly layered language. Amara used it to address Black-or-White Thinking, but another way orange is often used is as a support for rewriting a person's history to heal the timeline. That's how Judy used it.

Judy had a story about being ghosted. She felt nervous about reaching out to people for help, support, or even for friendship, because she was afraid they would abandon her for no reason, and without telling her why. Judy was afraid of being ghosted. She had a couple of examples of when that had happened to her in the past.

As she told me about them, she wove in a few mentions of when she thought she had ghosted other people. She felt horrible about it and said she deserved ghosting being done to her. I asked her to go back to one of the times where she had abandoned someone and to tell me about it in more detail.

As Judy told me her story, she started to realize there were some places where perhaps her narration of the story didn't quite match up with what she later came to know. For example, in one case, she hadn't completely ghosted the person. She had sent a note explaining why she did what she did (she'd left to take care of herself). That's not ghosting, since she'd given an explanation.

In another case, Judy realized her choice not to continue being friends with someone was because they had treated her pretty terribly. She was actually standing up for herself and her boundaries. Again, not ghosting.

As she looked back at these incidents, Judy was forced to admit to herself that she was not someone who just abandoned people when they were not convenient. She didn't "deserve" to be ghosted, she realized, yet she had been carrying around all that guilt anyway, and she had defined herself as someone who might abandon people.

As Judy reviewed her stories, she revised her understanding of her behavior in her story. She changed her story. She changed her timeline. She had a big shift in the present moment when she no longer saw herself as a person who abandoned other people when it was convenient. You might say Judy never was that person—but she believed she was that person, so she was that person.

When Judy updated her history by bringing in a more objective point of view, she also updated her beliefs about herself to something more accurate that truly served her. In this case, "serving her" meant helping her be kinder to herself and allowing herself to trust that she didn't ghost people, while also freeing her from an expectation (or fear) that others would treat her that way because she deserved it.

Judy's updated beliefs also meant she was able to see herself as a compassionate person who communicated with others in a caring manner, even when she was having personal difficulty. When she believes that's who she is, that's how she behaves. We are who we believe we are, right?

Judy's story is an example of how Color Thinking can heal our timelines and personal histories. As we heal our histories, we come to believe in our innate goodness, and thus our new stories help us be our best selves—who we believe we are!

Healing our timelines and rewriting our personal histories are examples of the work that is done when we choose to work with orange. We start with the story, then reinforce the new story with the future-state messages of orange. As Judy went on to reinforce her new story, she used orange for support.

Stay tuned. In the next few chapters (especially Chapter 11) there are lots more details on how to use color for support.

Color Thinking Exercise – Analyze Your Story

The exercise for this chapter is to analyze and understand how your story has shaped your life to this point. That's not a small exercise, is it? I know you can do it. Let me summarize the instructions here, so you don't have to reread the whole chapter above.

Put on your protective gear. Get yourself into the mindset that you are a research scientist. No judgment here!

Then read your story you wrote out in the previous chapter. Don't tell it, read it. Look for the assumptions, gaps, flaws, and outdated information. Highlight things. Mark it up. Use the list of questions above to make sure you've really analyzed your story.

Take a pink breather.

Next, analyze the impacts of your story. Using the impact questions above, look honestly and gently at how your story has been shaping your life and your experiences.

Then write up your findings, focusing especially on how you want to change your story.

***

You've done your research. You can take off the lab coat, goggles, and gloves now. But keep them handy, because you can use them any time you need to remember to be objective and non-judgmental. That goes for how you look at other people's stories, too. Just sayin'.

Make peace with the fact that you're no longer telling that particular old story. It's been your security blanket for so long, but now you've outgrown your blankie. If you're having a hard time giving up the old story, tell yourself it used to be your story, your blankie, but now you've realized it's a bit dirty and needs to go in the wash.

In the next chapter, we'll cut the blankie down to a small square anyway.

CHAPTER 6

STEP 3: FIND THE GEM

"Overwhelm is just a big pile of decisions that have to be made.
The only way out is to pull on a string and start making
decisions—one at a time."

—Anonymous

In the last chapter, you did a bunch of heavy lifting—the story analysis. I'm pretty sure you came up with lots of insights and impacts and new understandings. But you can't carry all that around with you everywhere. You need to distill it into something simple you can remember, something that really gets to the essence of it.

You need to excavate to find the gem.

It's okay if you take this part of the process a little less seriously than the previous two steps of telling and analyzing your story. It's even okay if you exaggerate for dramatic effect in this step. Overacting is encouraged. Poking a little fun and laughing is a great way to keep from getting embedded in the drama of it all—it's a way to stay objective, like when we dressed in the mental costumes of the scientist or detective.

Here's a recipe distilling your story process. Boil it down. Boil the old story, the automated pattern, down until you get to the essence. Can you summarize your pattern in one sentence?

Once you have your distilled pattern, fill in these blanks:

The pattern from my story is _____.

I think (or believe) _____, which makes me feel _____ and (do) _____.

See if you can come up with a simple "I statement" that sums it all up.

I know, I make it seem like there's a formula here. There isn't. Your distillation will be based on your insights. What we're trying to do here is get to the heart of the matter in some way. When you believe something is true, your story is evidence (for you). That belief makes you feel some emotions, and those emotions cause you to do (or not do) things that impact you in a way that doesn't serve you. That's the impact.

When you've distilled the old story, it will likely sound simple. Once you understand what's been going on for you, it is simple. Simple and profound and powerful. But a simple outcome is not the same thing as an easy process. If it takes you a little while to excavate your gems, be patient. I've included some case studies in Chapter 13 so you can see how other folks have worked this out.

Let me walk you through a couple of examples now, from the stories you've heard so far—complete with dramatization.

Remember Jordan? When he is excluded from something, Jordan makes everything about Jordan. He believes the only possible explanations are that he is either not good enough, or nobody loves him. As a result, no matter which explanation he chooses, he loses. He feels terrible about himself—hurt, unworthy, and unloved, which makes him defensive, angry, judgmental, and not very pleasant to be around. Jordan's gem? *I just suck.*

Let's try Jenna. Jenna is convinced that if something good happens it has to be followed by something bad in order to balance it out. She's got tons of evidence which she believes backs up her story. She believes she's doomed to a limited quantity of goodness in her life, which makes her feel trapped, so she doesn't really even try anymore. What's the point? Jenna's gem? *I'm cursed.*

Let's also revisit Judy from the last chapter. Judy was nervous about reaching out to people for help, support, or friendship. She was afraid of being ghosted. She had some examples where it had happened, but she had a big story about how she had abandoned other people and she believed she deserved it. Judy's gem? *I deserve to be ghosted.*

Those are good examples of the "sounds simple" principle—viewed from the outside, and because of the way I told their stories, these distillations seem pretty obvious. But imagine you are inside the story. Can you see how it might be hard to get to the essence, especially if you really believe you're cursed or you suck?

If you want to have a hope of seeing your way out of this paper bag of your old story, you need to stay objective, and you need to look for the cracks in the logic. You need to be able to say, "That thing I believe... what if it isn't true?"

It can really help to talk this through with someone you trust. Give them permission to check you on your assumptions, to ask you questions, to point out some of the impacts. They don't need to have the answers, they just need to prompt you with a few questions. It only works, though, if you do trust them and are willing to be vulnerable.

Once you have your gem, you still don't get to beat yourself up with it. That's never going to be okay in my book. And this is my book. So give that option up right now. Pummeling yourself has never gotten you the results you want, has it? It doesn't make you do better, be better, or work harder. It only makes you feel like shit. So don't do it anymore. Stop being mean to my friend!

Now that you have your gem, you can realize it is a gem, a precious insight that will unlock powerful transformation. Isn't it gorgeous?

Color Thinking Story – Helene

Helene is a client of mine who came to me with several decisions she had to make: Where to live, whether to change jobs or careers, when to make changes, etc. She had a lot of decisions teed up, and she felt overwhelmed. She wasn't making any decisions at all. She would analyze and analyze and analyze—she'd overthink everything, trying to figure out what she *should* do. And then she would stop analyzing and try to figure out what she *wanted* to do. She'd go back and forth between *should* and *want*. She'd try to move on to a different decision, thinking maybe that would be easier. Nope. Back into overwhelm.

The quote about 'overwhelm' at the beginning of this chapter is one of my favorites. I wish I knew who said it because I'd love to meet them and give them credit for their brilliance. I use that quote all the time because, the truth is that when you're overwhelmed, you just have to start somewhere and make one decision. Just one. And feel relief. Then make another one and feel the relief. You keep going with making decisions one at a time until you feel more relieved than overwhelmed. Once you feel a bit of relief, it gets easier and easier to make more decisions—then suddenly you're no longer overwhelmed.

As Helene and I talked about the pile of spaghetti sitting on her decision plate, we finally got to the essence of her story: "I don't know whether I should listen to my head or my heart when I make these decisions, so I keep going back and forth between the two. That's what's really got me paralyzed: I can't decide."

Of course, the more Helene told herself that she couldn't decide, the more true it became. It became her gem: *I can't decide.*

I call this type of indecision dithering. Or pinballing. Once we knew Helene's gem, the essence of the story, we could figure out what to do. I'll continue her story a little later on.

Color Thinking Exercise – Find Your Gem

I'm seeing a pattern here. Do you see it, too? These Part 2 chapters are mainly instructions for the work. Instead of repeating all those instructions here in the exercise section, I'll give you a summary, in case you're one of those people who wants to read the whole book first, then come back and do the work.

Look through your story analysis from the previous chapter and extract the essence, the fundamental pattern of the story. What is the core belief? How does it make you feel? How do those emotions make you act? Excavate until you find your gem, your "I statement"—because, yes, you do have to make this about you!

More direction for this process can be found in the main chapter text above.

***

In this chapter, we covered how to distill your story down to its essence. The moral of the story. The representative piece of your blankie. The core belief that has been holding you back. The gem—the precious insight that will help you make big changes.

In the next chapter, we'll find out what color that gem is!

CHAPTER 7

STEP 4: PRESCRIBE YOUR COLOR

"Show me a miracle, I wanna believe

Show me a miracle, Show me the real me

Give me a miracle"

—Alan Parsons, lyrics of *"Miracle"*
from the album, *The Secret*

In this chapter, we're going to find the color you'll be working with through the rest of the book. That's the color of your gem!

I know it may be tempting to pick a color you like, maybe even your favorite color. But that might not be what you need. As the Rolling Stones sang—and I'm paraphrasing—even when you don't get what you want, you might end up with what you need. I'm going to ask you to be open, maybe even to be surprised. Who knows? You might get a color you don't start off liking but end up having a pretty decent relationship with at the end.

Okay, so you aren't going to just pick a color you like. The color you need will actually pick you, and it's going to be based on where you are now (which is the diagnosis part) and where you want to be (which is the prescription part). I think it's pretty cool that those two are the same color—it has a symmetry that resonates. It's a whole solution. Holistic. I know spelling it *wholistic* is not correct, but it would be better if it were because it would be a reminder of the intent, and *wholistic healing* would make sense. But I'm not in charge of that stuff.

Getting back to choosing your color... Here's how you're going to do it. You'll go to the reference material in Chapter 14 and read through the Current State descriptions for the colors and pick the one that resonates the most with you in terms of Your Thing. The Current State is a description of the saturated, shadowy, negative aspects associated with a particular color. You're going to refer to your gem and your analysis and your emotions as you do this—those are like your symptoms. When you find a Current State that resonated with your gem, look in the color column and that's your preliminary diagnosis color.

We will confirm the diagnosis with a couple of tests.

The first test is to read through the Future State description associated with your diagnosis color. The Future State descriptions represent the infused, positive aspects of each color. You want to make sure the description is what you crave. In most cases, it will be spot on, because you crave the antidote for your current symptoms, right? Of course, you do. But in some cases, you might find the wording of a different Future State really calls to you. That's totally okay, because this is YOUR personal choice. You can use your emotions, intuition, and desires to validate. It's all about you—there is no one size fits all, remember? Do you need to update the diagnosis color? Go ahead. It's up to you.

The second test is to check the color against your own color vocabulary to make sure the meanings and understandings are close enough for you to be able to work with that color. If not, you will have to decide how to adjust the diagnosis. You might want two or four colors, which is fine. There are layers, and you can do this again and again. But choose one for now. You can't get it wrong. Trust me. Just use your intuition and pick one.

The whole point is to come up with the color that represents the messages that resonate the most. It doesn't mean you like that color the best. I'm sorry, it just doesn't. Hey, when you're done, you can throw it away if you want.

Color Thinking Story – Revisiting Old Friends

Let's look at some of the stories we've already talked about and take them into the Diagnose and Prescribe phases.

Jordan

Let's go back to Jordan ("either I suck or you don't love me"). You already know he chose pink. He completely resonated with feeling unloved or hurt. He also realized he was being needy and clingy when he made everything about him. He felt vulnerable—and not in a good way—because his view of himself was dependent upon how others thought about him. More accurately, his view was dependent upon what he **thought** other people thought of him, which was all based on the story he was making up in his own head. He didn't feel loved and he didn't have true self-confidence—and he craved both. He wanted to be in the space where he felt just fine about himself, where he was open enough to recognize he didn't need to read into people's motivations. He wanted to believe he could trust the people he loved, and trust that they loved him.

By the way, pink was not his favorite color—it still isn't. He wasn't surrounded by pink as a normal thing. When he started using pink as a support, it stuck out as a glaring reminder (if pink can be glaring) that he needed to change his thinking.

Jenna

Then there's Jenna the Cursed. Jenna was so afraid something bad was just around the corner that she could barely take any action beyond survival. She felt trapped by fate, history, karma, and past traumas. By the way, she also knew she was caught in a family history of alcoholism—she was the adult child of two alcoholic parents. She eventually came to see she had adopted her parents' way of thinking when she was very young. She was trapped in that chaotic, traumatic life. What she really wanted was to break free of that history of family trauma, to heal from the past. She wanted to have a radically new way of thinking. She didn't want to live in a scarcity mindset. She wanted to believe there was an abundance of wonderful things waiting just around the corner—things besides shoes waiting to drop. That's all orange.

Amara

Amara was the lucky one! She was there when the volcano of Color Thinking was born. She got to choose her favorite color, orange. Sometimes it's the luck of the draw, I guess. If you're thinking, "Hey, that's not fair!" then you might want to look at blue. Just sayin'.

Color Thinking Exercise – Your Diagnosis and Prescription

Here are the instructions for this step in a nutshell. Get out your journal or the workbook. Open up this book and go to Chapter 14. Read through the Current State stuff and find the one description that best describes where you are in relation to Your Thing. You might even find your gem in the list. Write that color down as your diagnosis.

Next, read the Future State description for that color. Is it what you crave? If yes, you have your prescription.

If you're the kind of person who wants to review all your options—and there's no judgment here, then run through these two tests until you're happy with your color:

Test 1 – Read through all the Future State descriptions to find the one you crave the most. Check it against the Current State for that color—is this color a better match?

Test 2 – Look back at your own color vocabulary. Does the color you chose pass the translation test into your own color language? Can you work with the understanding of the color from Chapter 14, or does this color mean something completely different to you? If you can't work with this color, don't force it. Find one that aligns with your color language.

Run through the tests until you can pick one color. Just pick one. That's your color for this story we're working on. Say hi!

***

In this chapter, you discovered the color of your gem. Next we're gonna work with it. Any questions? (I can't help but hear David S. Pumpkins say that—which is totally gonna date this whole book—and identify me as a fan of SNL and Tom Hanks. If you're not familiar, you can always Google it.)

I hope you do have questions because we're going to go swimming in questions in the next chapter.

CHAPTER 8

STEP 5: INTERRUPT WITH COLORFUL QUESTIONS

"Question Thinking... takes on an age-old issue—our ability to be in charge of our own thinking... and then guides us in designing new questions for getting better results. QT helps us do this mindfully, rather than reactively, leading to more astute choices for productive outcomes, even under pressure."

—Marilee Adams, PhD

You've done a lot of work on your pattern so far— and you've nailed it. You know your story, and you know how it has impacted you. You know you want to change it, and you know what you crave. You've picked the color you're going to use for your Color Thinking work. Wouldn't it be wonderful if that were enough? For some lucky few, that might be the case—and if that is you, I am truly very happy for you!

For the rest of us, we have a little more work to do. Our patterns are our patterns for a reason. Our patterns are what we do when the going gets tough and the autopilot kicks in. Our patterns are our own personal Groundhog Day story —even when we know they are there, and we know we don't want the same ending, we STILL repeat the pattern. How messed up is that? We call it self-sabotage, and we might believe we are doomed to repeat the same mistakes over and over—in fact, that might even be part of our story. I know it was part of mine— was some kind of special snowflake for whom the rules of logic didn't apply, and I was sure I would stay in the same endless loop forever. It was my pattern.

There's pretty much no way around it. We need to shock that pattern and interrupt it—mid-sentence. How rude! *Pattern, stop talking! Shush! Hush! Zip it! Stop!* You can Google some annoying Shush gifs to get the idea.

Remember, your brain is running this pattern because it is trying to protect you, be efficient, and save energy. Your brain doesn't think it's hurting you. I'm talking about your brain (especially the primitive part) as if it has a will of its own, but it's probably more accurate to think of it programming running in the background, maybe like early AI. That's more accurate, but not as fun.

I like to create characters for each part of my brain and give them speaking parts. It can get a little crowded on stage, but it does help me to break down the illusion that my brain should be running the show. I tend to make the cast like an SNL skit. It's more fun that way.

In one skit, my primitive brain is a very young girl who is trying to make me a soufflé, because she loves me (and wants me to eat). She really wants to do something nice for me, but a soufflé is a bit beyond her current abilities. What she ends up giving me are scrambled eggs and a wrecked cartoon kitchen—and I get to clean it all up! Her intentions are so sweet, but what a mess. Bless her heart (in full-on Southern there.)

That whole cooking show skit is a reminder that you're going to have to step in, be the grown-up, and manage your brain at this point. The management tool for this step is a pattern interrupt. Simply put, because your brain is involved, you're going to have to disrupt your thought patterns. You can't just jump into action and start doing different things. You have to do the thought work first, because if you don't your brain will revert to autopilot, and you'll notice your actions aren't effective and you've slid back into old habits. Same patterns, same results.

You have to change the way you *think*, and the most effective way to do that is to completely change your frame of reference. The easiest way to change that is with powerful questions that make you think with your cerebral cortex, the part of the brain in charge of executive function, the grown-up stuff. You need questions that will get past your cognitive dissonance defense measures and hit confirmation bias head-on, so you have a fighting chance to see things differently.

There are three tricks I love to use on my brain because I can't just tell her she's wrong. It doesn't work. My brain is a cunning negotiator, a sneaky distractor, persistent as a two-year-old and bossy as hell. She can pretty much convince me to her side—or wear me down—if I'm not wary. So I absolutely need to trick her, and I don't feel bad about it at all. I do it by asking questions in a specific way.

Trick #1: *What if...?* —Asking a question starting with *What if...?* is a great way to start off with a distraction. *What if...?* is like a saying, *Look, a puppy!* because it circumvents the whole confirmation bias thing and doesn't allow my brain to go to negation. Instead, *what if...?* invokes curiosity. *Huh, what if...?* A really good *What if...?* question is like getting a jolt of electricity, a shock. *Oh, what if something new and different is true?! Let's think about that!* Sure, my brain will lean toward what she already knows, but her curiosity will make her explore.

Trick #2: *How can...?* – My super helpful brain (the cerebral cortex) loooooves to solve problems. So when I phrase a question as a request to help solve a problem, she just jumps right in. *How can we...?* is the magic question that revs up the problem-solver brain, who takes over and does the shushing of the survival brain for me.

Trick #3: Make it a barrage – As soon as you have the answer to one question, follow up with another. Pelt your brain with powerful, interesting questions that tear down the defenses, open doors, and induce perspective-changing wonder.

Using thought-provoking questions as a tool to change the patterns of our thinking is not new. Great leaders, educators, and coaches do it all the time. Questions are one of the best self-coaching tools out there. Questions are really, really powerful when used right.

There are (at least) three things that matter when using questions as a pattern interrupt:

1. How you ask the question matters – Your mental tone of voice matters. If it's accusatory or condescending or infused with any kind judgment, it won't be effective. There is no need to be offensive because that will trigger being defensive, right? You don't have to have any agenda other than curiosity. Asking with an open mind invites hearing with the same openness. Sure, sometimes I use humor and drama when I'm asking questions, but it's a fine line to walk. As long as it sounds like a learning question and not a judging question, it's probably okay.

2. Which questions you ask matters, too – The better the question, the bigger the opportunity to shift. In the exercise section below, I give a list of some of my favorite all-purpose questions. In Chapter 14, you'll find a list of questions by color, designed to open your mind up in just the right way, tailored for what you crave—and who doesn't like a good tailoring job? I'm giving you some of my preferred tricks for how you phrase the questions, but I want to add you should stay away from *why* and *why not* questions, because your brain already has a pattern answer for those types of questions.

3. How you answer the questions probably matters most of all – Honestly. Answer honestly. Answering how you think someone else wants you to answer doesn't help. You want to discover what's going on inside your own head. You can't do anything until you find out what's going on in there. If you want to change your perspective, you have to be able to see. You don't need to judge yourself for your answers, either. Everything is open to change. Oh, and pay attention to the answers. There's a lot to learn from them. The answer is within you. Someone else might help you see and understand them, but they can't tell you the answer. Your brain wouldn't believe them anyway.

To repeat, your pattern interrupt is going to be a series of questions. You want to start by asking questions about your gem because that's the most focused part of your story. The idea is to change your perspective— *Maybe this gem isn't so valuable after all. Maybe it isn't accurate, isn't all there is. Maybe it isn't even true... Maybe it's a fake!* You've been duped! You've been robbed!

That's an example of a change in perspective.

After you've focused on your gem, you might want to start in on your story and see if you can find the weak spots to ask questions about. Maybe some of the stuff you've used as evidence to support your story and the conclusions isn't as great a fit as you used to think. Your story has been the house you've been living in for a long time. Perhaps some of the framework that once seemed like such a strong foundation has been eaten away by termites. One good kick might make the whole thing come tumbling down... or at least some renovation might be required.

Select pattern-interrupting questions that fit for you, based on your color (and your diagnosis and prescription, of course!). Chapter 14 includes lists of starter questions for some colors. Ask them, think about them, write down your answers. Feel free to tweak the questions, add your own questions, and follow any train of thought that seems like it might be productive.

I'll be honest. When I work with someone to come up with their questions, I start with the questions in the lists in Chapter 14, but I also come up with new ones I find by using my intuition. I have a knack for finding the weak beams of an old thought structure, and so I tailor the questions to expose them. I keep poking until I find the rotten wood. I tend to follow the strong emotions and the tears—the scent of the onion! The more I practice this, the better I get at it. That'll work for you, too.

Listen to what you have to say as you answer the questions. Notice the "old" perspective and see if you can change it. You'll know you've succeeded when you can recognize there's a distinct possibility that some of the things you have believed up until today might not be true. There might be one or two (or more!) weak beams holding up your story. Just find the weak points. We'll do demo and reno in the next chapters.

Color Thinking Story – Trina

Trina came to Color Thinking at a time when she was exhausted and almost crippled with self-doubt. She had been traveling for work almost non-stop for months. Here's her story in her own words.

I'm a fixer. I prove my worth by making everything okay for everyone else. I can be a conduit and give the love and healing people need.

I have a difficult time connecting to or expressing anger. I hate being misjudged or misinterpreted or misunderstood. I don't like public attention—there's too much judging involved. It's devastating. I'm prone to self-blame and I can allow bullies. Those are some of the dynamics of being a woman working in a man's world.

I need healthier boundaries, protection, and safety. I'm using too much of my own energy.

I feel like I'm using the wrong tank to provide my energy—I'm using MY tank. I'm using up all of my energy second-guessing myself, working harder, proving myself. But I'm not even sure I trust myself.

Here's an example. A few years ago, I was caught in a natural disaster. Afterward, I was safe. I had resources, contacts, and skills to be helpful. So, I didn't think—I just jumped in and started doing what I knew needed to be done. It made an impact. The disaster got a bunch of news coverage, and the things I had been doing got some positive publicity. I didn't seek it out; it just happened. There were a couple of men who were upset I got publicity and they didn't. They needed the publicity for their political careers. I didn't. They said terrible things to me. They were bullies. I didn't feel safe, and it caused me to question my motives. Was I really trying to do good? I feel like I have PTSD from that event—not the disaster itself, but the aftermath and the judgment and constantly questioning myself.

Analysis of Trina's Story

As we analyzed her story—made the diagnosis and prescription—we discovered there were some conflicting details in her story. Can you see them?

She was working so hard to make sense of the conflicts, and it was exhausting.

She knew her motivation: She is a good person and wanted to do good. She wanted to make things better for other people. But Trina didn't feel safe because her motivations were questioned, she was misjudged, and she was misunderstood. Her boundaries were crossed.

And she was also taking responsibility for allowing the bullies to bully her!

As we talked through her story, she realized she bought into the politicians' version of events and incorporated it into her story. Her own narrative of how she handled herself during the disaster didn't serve her.

Trina's Diagnosis

She currently feels threatened, bullied, weak, and defensive. She's exhausted and full of self-doubt. She does not feel safe.

Trina's Prescription

She craves security and safety. She wants to be free from bullying and she wants to feel strong, powerful, and committed. She wants to be able to make a difference without constantly questioning herself. She wants to take better care of herself so she is happier and has the energy to do more.

Trina's Gem

"I'm flowing (energy) from the wrong tank."

Trina's Color

"I want to work with red."

Trina's Questions

The questions didn't come all at once. They were honed by asking one question, answering it, and then digging for the next layer. This is pretty much how Trina's self-dialogue went:

What would love do? Love would find a way to take care of me and to be able to help others.

How has flowing from the wrong tank served me in the past? I was able to control situations and get things done more quickly.

How is it not serving me now? I'm exhausted. I second-guess myself. I doubt my motives. I don't take care of myself; I don't pay attention to boundaries.

How is it limiting me now? I'm not tapping into Source, so I'm not a conduit. I worry about whether I'm doing good. I hold back on what I could be doing.

Who would I be if I weren't limited? Oh my gosh, I could do so much more. And I wouldn't be doubting and blaming myself all the time. I think I could do more and be less exhausted! And happier and healthier.

How can I tap into Source and use it for good? I don't think you can tap into Source and use it for anything other than good. I think I just need to trust myself.

What do I need to do to use the right tank at the right time? I need to remember that I am inherently good and can trust myself. I am safe.

* * *

We will follow up with Trina and what she did next later on, but do you see how each question leads to better and better questions?

Color Thinking Exercise – Your Pattern Interrupt

Here are the instructions for your pattern interrupt. Get out your journal or the workbook. Open up this book to Chapter 14 and find the questions for your color, or tweak questions from the list of General Anytime Questions below. Feel free to add your own awesome questions. You get to decide which questions to use, based on what opens up the doors to show you your thinking.

Answer the questions honestly. Look at how you've been thinking. Look for the weak points in the structure of your gem and your story. What are they? Write them down. Aim for a change in perspective that opens the door to rewrite your story with a better ending.

What's your new perspective? Write that down, too.

General Anytime Questions

- What if it's just not true?
- What if there is nothing wrong?
- What am I grateful for?
- What would feel better?
- How could this be different?
- How could I make this whole thing easier?
- How is this perfect?
- How can I live my best life?
- What if there's something here for me to learn?
- What can I learn from this?
- What little things could I do differently?
- How can I use this?
- How can I add Joy, fun, love, light, etc.?
- What would love do?
- How am I making this harder than it is?
- What if I've been wrong all along?
- What would change everything? How would things change?
- What if the exact opposite of my gem is true?

***

We use powerful questions to interrupt and disrupt our old patterns of thinking. You can use questions that are homed in to address facets of your specific color, or you can choose questions from the General Anytime

Questions list, or you can create questions following your own internal wisdom, curiosity, and intuition.

When you've interrupted your old pattern, we'll move in a new direction. In the next chapter, you'll decide which direction to go, draw yourself a map, and build yourself a wagon to haul your ass there.

CHAPTER 9

STEP 6: REDIRECT

"Start telling a better-feeling story about the things that are important to you. Do not write your story like a factual documentary, weighing all the pros and cons of your experience, but instead tell the uplifting, fanciful, magical story of the wonder of your own life and watch what happens. It will feel like magic as your life begins to transform right before your eyes..."

—Abraham-Hicks

How you talk about what you want is a big part of how you chart your new course. You can't keep telling the same old story and expecting things to change. You have to tell your story in a different way or tell a new story altogether.

Okay, now we get into the fun stuff! We get to play with what we want. We get to dive deep into what you said you craved—your future state. This is all about aligning with the infused, positive aspects of your color.

Here's the thing. What we want won't happen just because we want it. It can't... not if we don't believe it can. So we have to make-believe. No, not pretend. *Make-believe* means to make our brains believe something is possible, even probable, and eventually believe that what we want is not only possible for us, but an absolute certainty. We have to make a belief.

If your brain is accustomed to believing something isn't possible, then, yes, it's going to take a bit of work to make it believe what you want and need it to believe. Now that you've interrupted your pattern—essentially turned off the autopilot—you have to take the controls and start steering. Obviously, you don't want to keep going in the same direction, so you're going to have to chart a new course. And to do that, you've got to settle on your destination.

This process is like when I was teaching Nic, my dog, to sit. First, I had to show him what I wanted him to do. He wanted to make me happy, but he was a little confused and a lot more interested in what HE wanted to do. I had to persist. I had to reward him when he got it right—or even close to right. It was such a wonderful feeling when he sat as requested the first time, then looked up at me with big, brown, loving eyes, virtually asking me, *Did I get it right?* Then next time, poof, back to the old behavior. I had to repeat the exercise over and over, for a prolonged time period. I had to be consistent in what I asked and how I asked it—no letting things slide. I had to create opportunities to reinforce what I wanted. Over and over. Persistent and consistent. Then one day, I realized that sitting was the new normal. No struggle. He even sits automatically when we're out on a walk and I stop. He's so well behaved. Nic loves it and I love it. And life with Nic is just so much easier.

So that's what you do with your brain. It's training. It can be a workout. But the steps are pretty straight forward. Each step is a wheel of a cart that is gonna haul your ass on your transformation journey.

The Cart

In this metaphor, you need all four wheels to get where you're going.

Wheel 1 – Direction

First, pick the direction in which you want to travel. Hey, you've already done that! Woohoo! You already know which direction you want to head because you described your future state and what you crave when you prescribed your color. The Future State descriptions—the prescriptions—listed in Chapter 14 are engineered to help you express how you want to feel. The emotions you desire are your direction.

By the way, we are very inclusive when it comes to emotions. You aren't stuck with only the 12-crayon box of emotions (happy, sad, angry, joyous, etc.). Nope, you can choose any emotional crayon you want. Want some examples? Edgy, boisterous, rambunctious, stifled, helpless, curious, valued, courageous, creative, sensitive, grateful, astonished, vulnerable, desperate, humiliated, valuable, energetic. See? Lots of options! If you can put the word "feel" in front of it and use it in a sentence, I'm cool with it—as long as *you* know what it means.

Wheel 2 – Destination

Second, choose a destination. Your job now is to put that desired feeling into an experience. You're gonna need a goal. It's got to be pretty specific, because it's a destination. Describe your goal as a way you can experience success. Your goal is a situation in which you feel how you want to feel, achieve what you want to achieve. Decide what you want, and make it really clear, so you can communicate it to your dog brain, and so you won't forget it as you're traveling along unfamiliar roads.

Go back to what you wrote for your future state—your prescription—and turn that into a goal. The goal is your next destination on your journey. For example, if you said you want to feel heard, set a goal where you can know you were heard by people who are important to you (maybe your siblings) or in a specific context (such as during office meetings).

If you've had training in setting SMART goals, I'm pretty sure I would like you to set it aside for now. A SMART goal is **Specific** (Okay, keep that); **Measurable** (Hmmm, you don't need metrics, but you do need a way to know that you've arrived at your goal. That could be covered by the specifics.); **Achievable** (Well, no, because if you keep it to what you believe is achievable right now, you're gonna stay where you are.); **Realistic** (Phhht. Same as achievable. But you have permission to put a little bit of reality in here. Use common sense. Like, why set yourself up to write a book by age 15 if you're already at least 16?); **Time-bound** (Whatever. Yes. You can say what you want by when.)

So we can't go with just the SMART formula. Turn off any corporate or project or performance or other goal-setting programs. For setting your goal, just use your own version of uncommon sense and fill in the what and where, by when, and who might be involved details. Don't worry about how.

Here's an example of a non-SMART goal: I will publish this book by June. That's pretty specific. Do I need a metric? Nope. Pretty easy to tell if I do it or not. Does it feel doable, achievable, realistic? It's a stretch, a big one, but doable. Do I know the when? Yes.

Here's another non-SMART goal example: Amara might choose to come up with an orange idea every single time she recognizes black-or-white thinking is happening. Your goal doesn't have to be brilliant; it just has to be different.

Wheel 3 – Drive

The third step is to identify your **drive**. So, let's talk about **Why**. We can't forget the why. Simon Sinek says to start with why. We're not starting there, but we sure don't want to forget it. I want to thank Donald Miller, of StoryBrand and Business Made Simple University, for the inspiration on how to make finding your why a pretty simple exercise.

We get to use our asking-powerful-questions skill again, but this time you DO get to ask "why?" Answer these questions, starting with "because…," and zero in on your most compelling answers.

- Why am I doing this?
- Why do I want to make a change?
- Why do I want to feel better?
- When things get uncomfortable, or confusing, or maybe even a tad difficult, why will I persevere?

How do you know your goal is compelling? It will probably make you cry. (Donald Miller doesn't say that, but I do!) You'll cry because it's meaningful to you, because it's so powerful.

If you need a hand getting started, you can look back at your story analysis. Your answers about why could simply be because you don't want your current state anymore because you crave your future state. But there could be more. Is there more? For me, personally, my why almost always comes down to this pervasive theme: *If I feel better, I am better, and I want to be my best.* That's my why. You want to find the answer that will motivate and sustain you—and is pretty easy to remember.

What is your why? That's your drive. That's how you're going to power through.

Wheel 4 – Desire

And the final step is **desire.** To understand how desire fits here, let's talk about belief. It always seems to come back to beliefs, doesn't it? Well, the hints were placed along the way.

If you continue to believe what you believe about yourself, you aren't going to go anywhere new. You'll follow the same path and get to another version of the same destination. To get somewhere different, you're going to need to believe something different. What might that be? This takes some thinking. Don't worry about *how* you'll believe something new. That's covered in the next chapter. Right now, let's pick out your cart, then we can put the dog in front!

Look at what you believe now. Look at those weak timbers you identified in the last chapter. They need to go, no question. But what should you replace them with? What do you absolutely need to believe to be able to get to your goal? What do you need to believe about yourself to make it possible? That's where you start—with what you need to believe. But you might want just a little more. What would you like to believe? What do you wish you believed? What would feel amazing to believe? What would you absolutely *love to believe*? That's it. That's **desire.**

***

Direction. Destination. Drive. Desire. The four wheels of the cart, so to speak. We'll continue with training our dog brains to pull the cart in the next chapter.

FINAL NOTE: If you are someone who has no problems setting a goal, you can skip this paragraph. It's just a rant. But if you're having problems picking a goal, then read this to yourself—preferably out loud. It's a lecture. You don't have to be judgy as you read, but you do have to be firm:

What do you mean you don't know how to set a goal, that you can't be specific? How will you know you've arrived at your destination if you aren't specific? Now don't give me any wishy-washy bullshit here. Yes, you do have to be specific, you do have to have a goal, and, yes, you do know what it is. Being confused is an excuse. It's self-indulgent, and not in a good way. Being confused keeps you stuck right where you are—and you've got places to go, people to see. Pick a goal. It's not your last goal, it's your first! And, yes, you can still enjoy the journey. It's not a choice of either reach your goal or enjoy the journey. It's f*cking both! We don't need black-or-white thinking here! No either/or. It's both/and—and more! Pick something and practice the process. It will get easier. Trust me. Trust your intuition. You've got this.

Color Thinking Story – Jordan Continued

Let's take Jordan's story and talk through his redirection work. This part will be different for everyone, so his story is an example, not a model to follow. You have to pick what will work for you!

Jordan's Direction

I want to feel loved and self-confident, and open to explanations beyond my default *I suck* or *they don't care*.

Jordan's Destination

I want a new default. When I hear of something where I'm not included, I want my first thought to be, *Okay, I might be hurt, but I don't have to be. What is one possible explanation that has absolutely nothing to do with me?*

Jordan's drive

I'm sick of feeling like this, and I don't like how I behave. I want to be more loving and more lovable!

Jordan's desire:

I want to believe people can love me AND choose not to include me in everything they do.

***

Once Jordan said what he wanted to believe out loud, it didn't seem like that big of a stretch to him. In fact, it was pretty easy for him to catch hold of it and run with it. Sometimes it's as easy as that, but it isn't always the case, and we'll come up with some strategies around this in the next chapter.

Color Thinking Exercise — Chart Your New Course and Build Your Cart

Open your journal or go to the workbook. After reading this chapter, and maybe rereading it, write down the essence of your direction, destination, drive, and desire.

Direction – What's the future state you want to travel toward? This is the future-state emotion (or emotions) you crave. Go back to your prescription and pick the emotions that are most compelling for you. Start with *I crave...*

Destination – What's your goal? Do you know by when you want it? Who is involved? Make it specific enough that you'll be able to know when you've arrived! Start with *My goal is...*

Drive – Why do you want to change? What has not changing cost you? What will keep you going when you have doubts, are uncomfortable or confused, or when it's just kind of hard? Start with *Because...*

Desire – What do you need to believe about yourself to achieve the goal? What would feel amazing to believe? Start with *I would love to believe...*

***

The cart you built in this chapter? It's a dog cart. You're gonna train your dog brain to haul you to the next destination on your journey, which happens to be a construction site, where you're going to build a new belief. No hard hat required on this site!

CHAPTER 10

STEP 7: BUILD THE BEST BELIEF FOR YOU

"We're all mad here. You have to be a bit (or a lot) bonkers, mad, or crazy in the greatest way possible to accomplish something that really matters. The easiest thing is to let others criticize or not support your wild ideas. It takes your own internal total knowing to be strong—so it doesn't matter what anyone else says, believes, or does that isn't in support of your vision. You only look mad until it works. Then others could see it all along."

—Yanik Silver

Even though this chapter has "Build" in its title (which sounds a lot like work), it's still going to be fun. Yup, we're still in the fun stuff. Work can be fun. What? You didn't know that?

Your job here is to build a new belief or two (or more!) In the last chapter, you picked out what you want and need. That's your desire, remember? If you were able to get really specific, that's fantastic. But chances are, choosing the right new belief seemed a wee bit daunting, maybe even confusing. Heck, maybe it even bordered on unbelievable. I've got you. This is probably the most important piece of your puzzle to be able to solve, so let's set some time aside to dive deep and get this thing done right.

A few reminders: 1) Your beliefs in this specific area (Your Thing) are at least partially outdated—otherwise you wouldn't have chosen it as Your Thing. 2) Your outdated beliefs keep automatically taking you to the same old place, and you'd rather not return there *again*, thank you very much. 3) You can update your beliefs so they help you get where you do want to go (your destination).

Here's a funny thing—which should totally be a review by now, and hopefully you've found an amusing example or two in your own life: Beliefs don't have to be true. They can be absolutely ridiculous. You just believe them. You believe them because you've thought the same thoughts so many times they've become part of your programming. You've just stopped questioning them. You interpret the world around you to fit your existing beliefs, NOT THE OTHER WAY AROUND. There's an *ergo* in here somewhere. *Ergo* means *therefore*. Let's see: *Beliefs don't have to be true...* let's put the *ergo* here... *you can believe anything you want.*

You can choose to believe anything you want! People do it all the time. Look around at all the wackadoodle things people believe. Granted, they're wackadoodle by my standards, but that's the point! I'm not suggesting you need to believe that people from the future are planting population-control drugs in the chemtrails of the Airbus plane flying over your city. I'm only suggesting that you *choose* to believe something that will support you in becoming who you want to be, doing what you want to do, feeling how you want to feel, contributing what you want to contribute. Yeah, crazy shit like that. We're all mad here. Until it works.

By the way, I chose the quote at the start of this chapter because I kept seeing the phrase "we're all mad here" in different places as I was writing this book. I saw it in a journal I gave my niece for Christmas. It was carved on a piece of driftwood I received as a gift. It was in the quote I came across then put at the start of this chapter. You know, what a coincidence. I was going to use this quote in the next chapter, when I talk about signs. But then, I realized it needs to be here ... because your new beliefs require your own internal total knowing, even if at first it seems a bit mad.

I'm not naive enough to think you can just decide to believe something and—Poof! Voila! —you're now a believer. Nope. And that's where the work comes in—there's stuff we've gotta do to make the belief —to make-believe. You have to build your new belief, and you might need to pretend and act-as-if for a while. You'll definitely need to reinforce it and practice it.

The Chain Reaction

But first, I want to throw in another reminder, from way back in Chapter 2, where I talked about the general rule for emotions, which is *emotions are intense sensations usually caused by thoughts about our situations.* (Remember, this is the general rule, not one of the few exceptions.) Another way to say this is *what we feel is the direct result of what we think.* Thoughts create emotions. This is all part of the bigger chain reaction of human behavior, and if we understand how it works, we can use it to take our new beliefs out for a test drive to make sure they're going to work for us.

To review the chain reaction of human behavior... Something happens. We have pre-existing beliefs, which influence what we think about the something that happened. Those thoughts trigger emotions. Our emotions drive our behavior, our actions. The actions we take are what ultimately determine our outcome, or results, such as whether or not we achieve our goals.

This chain reaction probably seems pretty obvious when it's laid out like that, right? It's the secret behind *The Secret*, and by that, I mean it's the explanation for how the Law of Attraction works. If we could double-click on the statement *your thoughts create your reality* to see the detail behind it, we'd see the chain reaction. And if we went up a level, we'd see the summary statement *your beliefs create your reality*.

Since we now know we CAN change our thoughts and our beliefs, with a little work and some practice, we know how to solve the equation to change our reality. We just need to look at the chain reaction—what you'd see if someone said, "Show your work"—to make sure it goes as planned.

Huh. That might be kind of new for you. I'd better give you an example and show *my* work. If this isn't new to you (meaning you've done tons of this type of thought work before with your own coach or with a thought model or whatever), feel free to pick my work apart and correct it. But use your inside voice.) Let's use Jordan's current story as our example:

- **Jordan's Pre-Existing Beliefs** – There are only two possible reasons for me not to be included: Either I suck or you don't love me.
- **Something Happens** – His fiancé, Zoe, is invited to go on a trip with her mom.
- **Jordan's Thoughts** – I wasn't invited. It has to be because you don't love me. (Remember, Jordan sees only two possible choices, and I

suck doesn't seem to fit in this case. As a result, autopilot takes him to you don't love me.)

- **Jordan's Emotion** – Hurt (unloved, alone)
- **Jordan's Action** – He sits home alone, spinning in the story about how he isn't loved, and wondering why.
- **Jordan's Outcome** – He's miserable, lonely, and continues to feel unloved.

Jordan's belief that there are only two possible explanations means he doesn't even look for another plausible explanation. Autopilot takes him to *you don't love me.*

By the way, there are many other plausible explanations. Spoiler alert: He picked the wrong one! In the scenario above, Jordan sits at home and mopes, instead of doing something he would actually enjoy doing. Chain reaction. Rinse, repeat.

Building the Best Belief

Okay, to change the chain reaction, the best place to start is with our beliefs. So let's get on with building the best belief.

There's a methodical way to do this, to build a better belief and then test drive it. I like to start at the end of the story and work back up the chain, one link at a time, because a) it's easier, and b) it can save a bunch of rework. I'm smart *and* lazy, so I like to avoid rework. To work backward, we start at the end of the story. We are reverse engineering our success.

I'm having trouble deciding which pronoun to use here—*you* or *I*. There's a trick many non-fiction writers employ, which is to use the pronoun *you* in order to connect with the reader. I've pretty much just been talking to you, so I've been saying *you* where I mean you, and *I* where I'm talking about myself. No trick needed. But in this case, it sounds too much like a lecture to say *you*, so I think I'll go with... we, so we're in this together. You wouldn't need to know that, except the next section might not flow perfectly. Please forgive me. Back to the backward work.

Where do we want to end up? What are the outcomes we want? Our goals! Great. This is why our goals need to be specific.

What happens before that? We take action. How do we have to show up? What are one or two things we need to do to make our goals happen? Actions we need to take? We don't have to make full plans here; we just need some examples we can use for our testing.

What happens before that? We need to feel the right emotions, the ones that will enable us to take these actions. So how do we have to feel to be able to show up the way we want to show up to do the things we need to do?

And before that, what do we have to think in order to feel that way? What thoughts cause those emotions? We'll need to review this one at least twice because sometimes, we expect a thought to cause a specific emotion, but it doesn't. Therefore, we need to think the thought and see what emotion comes up. The awesome news is we can use our imaginations and trust the results—because our brains don't distinguish between real and imaginary when it creates emotional responses.

At the very beginning, what do we need to believe in order to be able to think those thoughts? That's what we're test-driving. Does this belief deliver? Does it take us where we want to go? Does it give us the thoughts and emotions we need to take the actions and get the outcomes? Does it start the correct chain reaction? If the answers are *nope*, we need to tweak something in the belief. If *yes*, then we're good to go on.

And that's the process.

Now let's take it out for a drive. You take the wheel. I'll sit here in the passenger seat. This is what you'll do in the exercise section for this chapter—you can pull out the worksheet or your journal and do this process right now, or you can think it through for now and write it down later. Ready? Let's start.

First, let's make sure you have the right new belief—the one that's gonna take you where you want to go. What's your goal again? Pull it out from the last chapter. While you're at it, grab your new belief so we can test it. Let me remind you this is supposed to be fun. Yeah, it might be a bit hard at first, but keep aiming for *this new belief is fun and feels good*.

What's your goal?

What are one or two things you might need to do to achieve it? Or, how do you need to show up? Or both.

What emotion do you need to feel to be able to show up and take those actions?

What thoughts do you need to think to feel those emotions? Double-check: Do those thoughts work? There's no formula for this part. It's a very personal thing. Only you can tell if the new thoughts will work. If not, tweak the thoughts until you get one that gets you to feel the right emotion.

What's your new belief? Does it work with the thoughts you need to start the chain reaction? You might need to tweak the wording of the belief.

I know this may be a bit confusing at first. I use this working-backward process for a lot of things. It's harder to describe than it is to do! Just give it a shot. Ultimately you can work the chain either way.

Here's a summary of the chain:

Belief —> Thoughts —> Emotions —> Actions —> Goal

Wanna Buy a Bridge?

Do you believe your belief? You might not. It might be quite a leap, a stretch, given where you are today. That's okay, I have a bridge to sell you. Actually, you can't buy this bridge; you have to build it. You might not want a bridge. You might want stepping-stones. You might want a step ladder, or an on-ramp or even training wheels. You need some type of help to get from here (what you currently believe) to there (what you want to believe), in stages you can realistically believe. Yeah, your belief has to be believable to you. Even if you don't believe it yet, you have to be pretty sure you can get there, somehow. Don't think about this too hard. It'll make your head hurt.

Let's try an example.

Jenna wants to believe she isn't cursed and that everything happens for a reason and for the greater good. Can she just believe that now? Nope. But she wants to believe it. So she builds a staircase. Her first step is *I want to believe everything happens for the greater good*. She will practice that and look for evidence to support it (more on that later). When this stepping-stone belief feels pretty solid, she'll move on to the next step, which for her is *It could be possible that I can find a good reason instead of the curse*. And then on to *I am choosing to think there is a good reason for everything that happens in my life*. That one is pretty important for her because when she's ready for that step, she's ready to admit she is the one choosing what she thinks. The next step, the one where she believes she isn't cursed, is an easy reach now.

Building your bridge is something you have to do for yourself. On *The Rainbow Onion* website (**therainbowonion.com/bonus**) there's a list of starter thoughts (like Mad Libs—remember them?) you can play around with to build your bridge, or staircase, or ladder, or whatever your heart desires to move you to your new belief. While you're at it, why not make your bridge fun?

You've got your new belief. You've tested it and, yes, it's the right one for you. You've got your bridge-like thingy if you need it. Now you just need to drive around in your new belief. What could possibly go wrong? Well, like Judy Robinson (and a bunch of others) said, your best strategy is to "accept the unexpected." Resistance is pretty much futile. Work the problem.

Why don't we plan on the idea that the unexpected will come up— accept it and build some support to get you through? Intention, willpower, and white-knuckling are not the ways to go. There's so much more *The Rainbow Onion* has to offer! I know I keep saying this, but this next part will be really fun!

Color Thinking Story – Jordan Continued Again

Jordan chose to work with pink. We already know that from the layers that we have peeled. But he couldn't just jump to his Future State of pink acceptance. He needed to build a bridge to get to his new pink thinking.

Let's take Jordan's story and talk through an alternative future. Oooh, an alternate timeline—I love those!

What if we take Jordan's pre-existing belief and tweak it a tiny bit to turn it into a bridge belief? What if we say there are *three* possible reasons for him not to be included, and the third is a mystery? That third reason could take him somewhere different and cause a very different chain reaction.

- **Jordan's New Possible Bridge Belief** – *There are three possible reasons for me not to be included:* Either I suck, you don't love me *or* X.

- **Something Happens (the Same Thing)** – His fiancé is invited to go on a trip with her mom.

- **Jordan's Thoughts** – *I wasn't invited. It has to be because* I suck, Zoe doesn't love me*, or the third reason.* I suck *doesn't fit. What could the third reason be?* Now we've given his brain a puzzle to solve! It's on a mission. He starts thinking of possible other reasons, comes up with several possibilities. He lands on a brand-new story that is quite plausible: *Zoe's mom wants to spend time with her daughter. They haven't had much together since Jordan and Zoe moved to a different state. Yes, and I actually want them to be able to spend time together! They'll probably even do some wedding planning.*

- **Jordan's Emotion** – *Happy for Zoe and her mom.*

- **Jordan's Action** – He makes plans to hang out with his friends and do things Zoe doesn't enjoy doing.

- **Jordan's Outcome** – He feels more connected to his friends, he gets to do stuff he doesn't usually do, and he gets to feel loving and happy for Zoe and her mom.

Jordan's bridge belief was a pretty simple tweak, and he could readily accept there might be a third reason he didn't know about. Once he started trying to solve for X, he discovered there were tons of possibilities, and very few of them had anything at all to do with him. What a huge relief! When we look at his story, we might be tempted to think *Duh There are lots of possibilities*. We can see them because we aren't operating inside Jordan's belief system—the one that only allowed for two possible explanations. Damn that black-or-white thinking!

Bonus Color Thinking Story – My Money (Fear) Story

I'll give you a bonus story in this chapter, as another illustration of the chain reaction and the role beliefs play in it.

After a bit of soul searching, I chose a money story to tell. I chose it not because I think money is the same thing as abundance. I don't. My money story is about fear, and fear has never made me a better version of me. Just the opposite, in fact. Perhaps, it's more accurate to say that this is a fear story, and money happens to play a part. By the way, if I had been working with Color Thinking back then, I would have chosen to work with yellow.

- **My Pre-Existing Beliefs** – I've had bunches, but the relevant one here is *I will always struggle with money*.
- **Something Happens** – An envelope comes in the mail from the IRS.
- **My Thoughts** – There are lots of them. They come in a tidal wave. Before I can coherently grab one, my survival brain has told me a

story of doom and gloom and back taxes and fines and, gasp, an audit.

- **My Emotion** – Fear
- **My Action** – Avoidance. I put the envelope down and don't even open it. (Hey, not everyone would do the same in this situation—that was my response at the time.)
- **My Outcome** – I stay afraid. When I finally open the envelope, I do owe some money and I've already missed the date to respond, so there's also a penalty, and I owe even more money.

True story. Thirty years ago, I was a young, inexperienced pup who had inherited lots of money beliefs from my parents, which were pretty much all around the idea that I was always going to struggle with money and never have enough. Those beliefs completely shaped the thoughts that clustered together to form the story and the ending. I held the belief that I would struggle with money, in spite of tons of evidence to the contrary (oh, you know, like the fact I had a well-paying job could be interpreted as evidence of something else). I either didn't see or misinterpreted evidence that supported my existing belief. (Confirmation bias!) Because I held a belief about struggling with money—outdated though it was—I made a bigger mess of that situation, so there was more to clean up... which I then used as evidence to continue to support my struggle belief. See the cycle?

The cleanup of that money (fear) belief did require me to take action, and it was all really hard work at the time. We've already seen that when I am afraid, I would rather avoid things than face them head on—at least the me of thirty years ago would! (I can proudly say it's not true of the me now, and do I ever have evidence to support THAT belief!)

But back to then. Because I didn't know about the chain reaction, I basically had to white-knuckle doing things, even though I didn't believe they would work. I had to do them because, you know, the IRS.

That's the hard way. I had a mentor who believed in me and who helped me through the two years it took to get everything cleaned up and my finances back on track. Thank goodness she also helped me see things differently and use those two years as evidence to support new beliefs. My new beliefs were: *I am not doomed to have money struggles*, *I am not a victim*, and *I am responsible for my own life*, which was way bigger than money!

When I look back at that situation, I see that if I had known about the chain reaction—how my beliefs were shaping my reality and I could change my thinking—it would have been so much easier, because I would have known to clean up my thinking first. And if I'd had also had Color Thinking and *The Rainbow Onion* process... well, if only!

Here's what the me of last year did:

- **My Updated Beliefs** – I am responsible (the related backstory belief is I keep good tax records, take care of my obligations, and/or correct mistakes.)
- **Something Happens** – An envelope comes in the mail from the IRS.
- **My Thoughts** – Yikes! (Because it's the IRS, right?) I wonder what's in the envelope. I'd better open it to find out, so I can take care of it.
- **My Emotion** – Capable. (It's a pretty neutral emotion.)
- **My Action** – Open the envelope. It's a notice that my California tax refund was applied to my federal taxes.

- **My Outcome** – I am responsible and everything is fine.

That's a pretty boring story. Not much drama at all. We like boring IRS stories. Correction: We LOVE boring IRS stories.

Color Thinking Exercise – Build the Best Belief for You

Before you start, let's invoke the power of your color. You chose it because you are craving the Future State, right? Take a moment and remember the aspects you really want and let them be the inspiration for your new beliefs. Pick up something in your color and have it near you while you do this exercise, so you're visually reminded to tap into the future state. Maybe even choose to write with the color.

Open your journal or go to the workbook. Let's redirect your thoughts, emotions and actions to support your new direction. You can do these in any order, but they must all support each other! I suggest you write in pencil, so you can erase and adapt as you take your belief for a test drive. If you don't want to work backward (like I do), go to the end of these instructions and work your way up to the start.

- **Write down your outcome** – Go get your goal from the last worksheet. That's the outcome you want.
- **Write down some actions to take** – What are one or two actions you need to take—or things you need to not do—in order to accomplish your goal (not the full plan) and/or how do you need to show up?
- **Write down the emotions you'll need to feel** – How do you need to feel to be able to show up and take the action you need to take?

You'll probably come up with several but pick the one emotion most important for you.

- **Write down the new thoughts you'll need to think** – What specific thoughts do you need to think to cause you to feel the emotion you need? Pick one thought and focus in on it to get the wording just right.

- **Write down your new belief** – What do you need to believe in order to think that thought?

- **Take it for a spin** – Think the thought you identified above. When you think that thought, what emotion comes up for you? Is it the emotion you need? Remember, this is very personalized—it has to work for you! If you think the thought but don't get the emotion you expected, tweak the chain until it comes out right. That's why you used pencil! When it comes out right, let's move on and see if you need a bridge.

- **Do you need a bridge?** – Check your new belief. How comfortable is it? Is it a stretch? You don't need to believe it 100% yet—we'll work on that next, but *could* you believe it? If you think believing it is just a matter of practice and awareness and gathering some evidence to reinterpret, then great. You don't really need a bridge. But if you think you might need an interim belief, then you probably want to come up with at least one bridge thought. If you think it might take a few steps to get to your new belief, pick an interim belief or series of beliefs that allow you to take gradual steps, like a staircase or a ladder or stepping-stones. Pick the imagery you want and draw it in your journal. Fill in what you believe now and what you want to believe, then design the transition beliefs.

(Remember, there's a list of sample bridge thoughts on the website.)

When you've finished, we'll move on to get ready to accept the unexpected.

***

In this chapter, we covered how the chain reaction works in your brain and how you can use it to your advantage to build and test a belief that will serve you, that will help you show up the way you want to show up, do the things that you want to do, and be the person you want to be.

We've spent a lot of time in Thinking and now we get to dig back into Color and add the two together to make the magic happen.

CHAPTER 11

STEP 8: PLAN THE MAGIC IN COLOR

"Radical self-care is quantum, and it radiates out from you into the atmosphere, like a little fresh air. It's a huge gift to the world. When people respond by saying, "Well, isn't she full of herself," just smile obliquely, like Mona Lisa, and make both of you a nice cup of tea. Being full of affection for one's goofy, self-centered, cranky, annoying self is home. It's where world peace begins."

—Anne Lamott, 2017 TED Talk

At the very least, this chapter tells you two things: How to get to your new destination (exactly what you do) and what you're going to need to support yourself along the way (your support and self-care). As Anne Lamott tells us in the quote above, true self-care is the opposite of selfish. I want to say this again and again, until we all believe it: Being our best selves is good for everyone. Remember that from here on out, please.

How to Get to Your New Destination

Your transformation is a journey. You absolutely, positively want to enjoy the journey. But you also want to make sure you reach your destination—your goal, which comes with a new belief and the new thoughts you need to think (all that stuff from the last chapter). I know, I know, I'm repeating myself, but it's important.

The big question is *How does your* new *belief become your* now *belief?* The answer is *the same way your old belief became your new belief— through repetition, practice, and evidence.* We can speed up the process by using what we've recently learned about how our brain works—and how to manage it.

Let's go back to teaching a dog to sit. What you're doing with your brain in a new chain reaction is a very similar process. You're the trainer, and the objective is to get your brain to sit automatically— aka to believe your new belief. So... you have to be conscious. You have to pay attention to what your brain is thinking and correct it when it goes off on its own back into old habits. You have to be the one in charge. You have to set the intention that you're going to train your brain to believe what you've chosen to believe. It's helpful to remind yourself why you've chosen the new belief and why you want to go through this whole thing (you know, your *why*).

Before you start, get your head on straight. Remember you're doing this with and out of love. This is super important. Things won't come out the way you want if you're constantly yelling at yourself, berating and pummeling yourself when you make a slip—because you will slip! You can't be judgmental and make yourself wrong for everything you've done in the past. You aren't trying to train your brain to cower in fear! It's also not going to help if you spend a lot of time blaming others or revisiting your old story. In fact, it's best if you spend most of your energy looking forward, not back. So, eyes front, and look through the lenses of love. Firm but gentle voice.

Now, to start, show your brain what you want—that's your new belief and the thoughts you want to think. You can add a few more thoughts that are aligned because it's nice to have a few in your pocket when you need them, but you don't need bunches. Simplicity is easier to remember. I like to write the thoughts down and put them all over the place so I have reminders. Sticky notes are awesome and—hint, hint—they come in colors (I include some tips about this in the support section later).

Pay a lot of attention to what you think. Actually listen to the thoughts you're thinking (that's the being conscious part). Are they in line with what you want to think? Here's a hint: Notice what emotions you're feeling. They can help you to tell whether the thoughts are on or off track (there are tips about this later, too—there are tips in the support section for lots of stuff, so I'm just going to stop saying that).

Recognize and reward your brain when it gets it right. That means giving yourself some internal love and celebration. Seriously, tell yourself you're doing a good job. You've got to be able to recognize when you're making progress.

Another way to reward your brain is to incorporate fun. That's the magic we'll talk about in the support section (okay, fine, *now* I'm going to stop talking about the support section).

One more way to reward your brain is to make sure it sees and interprets the evidence in ways that prove the new belief. The brain wants to be right! So intentionally look for new evidence, and probably re-work or reinterpret your chain reaction occasionally, to make the evidence fit the new belief. This might be a little uncomfortable at first, because of all the confirmation bias and cognitive dissonance stuff—another reason to keep your *why* handy.

You will need to correct your brain when it gets things wrong. Every. Single. Time. Gently, without yelling or punishing. It will happen, because your old beliefs and interpretations of evidence are habits, and you've been running on autopilot for so long. That's why it takes concentration to stay observant. If you find you're feeling the old emotions, look at your thoughts and deliberately rewrite them.

One nice thing is the fact that you can reason with your brain, unlike with a two-year-old or a German shepherd. You can explain to yourself where the breakdown happened, what you're trying to accomplish, etc. I have no idea if reasoning out loud helps enforce the new belief, but it does help to know that you don't sound silly talking to yourself. You can talk to your brain inside your head, though. Whether you use your inside voice or your outside voice, I choose to believe it does help to explain things to your brain - at least it is another opportunity to repeat the thoughts. See? That's how that evidence thing can work.

Be persistent. Be consistent. Keep going. Make up reasons to examine and reinforce. Build habits to help you think the new thoughts. Find evidence to support the new belief. Soon—sooner than you think—it will become automatic.

This works for your bridge or step-beliefs, too. Once you believe your interim belief, tell yourself *Great job!* then go back and teach your brain the next behavior. Build on your success.

That's the how. Hopefully it doesn't sound so mysterious now. Keep thinking the new thoughts. Think them enough times and they will become beliefs.

The next big question is *What happens when things don't go exactly as planned?*

Color Support and Self-Care

In the last chapter, I suggested we accept the unexpected and make support plans. That sounds a little oxymoronish, right? I mean, how can we plan for what we don't expect? The answer is we can't plan for every possible event, but we can create a pretty decent support system for the things we can expect. That's my version of the 80/20 rule. If you can plan and prepare for eighty percent of the stuff, you'll have a lot more energy left for the twenty that might happen—the exceptions. Hmm, maybe it should be *accept the exceptions*?

How do you do that? With your own special magic! Sure, it's work, but it's also magical, because the result is a transformation!

Here's the scenario: You're going on a journey. You're departing from your current situation and heading out toward your future state. You're taking your new belief—that's how you'll get there. There will be some bumps in the road, some unexpected turns along the way. There will be times when the journey seems amazing and wonderful and you can't believe all the beautiful scenery, the wide vistas in front of you. There will also be times where you're tired, you'd like to rest, and it seems very tempting to go back where you came from because at least it was familiar. Not wonderful, just familiar. You're also a little nervous about getting lost. What if it gets too dark to see? What if your new belief breaks down and you don't know how to repair it yourself? What if you come down with a belief cold or something? How are you going to handle such things when they come up?

You get prepared. Yes, we are finally here in the support section!

Let's put together a support plan for your transformation journey. You'll need to know what to pack, so let's make a list. You'll need an itinerary, a map, and something like a GPS. You'd probably like a how-to manual for handling basic things that might come up, the minor repairs. Having the right tools would also be handy, right? Great. You already have some of these things. We just need to pull everything together. We'll pack your support in a conceptual magic box—decorated in your color!

Let's get a bit more specific about what goes in your box.

Your Color Toolbox

Gather the things you already have—your goal, your *why*, your new belief, any thoughts you would like to think. Strictly speaking, the master copy stays in your box, but you're going to need to put up a lot of signs to remind yourself where you're headed. You'll need to put them up everywhere, so you can see them when you need them. One of the best ways I've discovered (so far) to do this is to write the new belief and the new thoughts on sticky notes and put them up around the house, on your dashboard, maybe on your desk or computer monitor or mirror—anyplace you'll see them throughout your day. Incorporate your color, by using colored Post-its or paper, printing using a colored font, or write them out using your color.

Use every opportunity you can to incorporate your color. It's part of your new language. It's a visual reminder of your entire journey. You are the color you chose (or that chose you), and you will become the future you crave to be. Your color is your own magic.

You can use your color to create your talisman. In case you aren't familiar with the idea of a talisman, it's something that has a particular power and energy for the possessor. (That's you!) It is magically charged with the force it's intended to represent. When you chose your color, or when it chose you, it became your talisman, charged with the force of the future you crave.

Here are some sample ways to incorporate your color into your daily life:

- **Add your color to your surroundings** – Put up images or artwork that feature your color. Paint a wall. Change your screensaver.
- **Hold objects that are your color** – You can layer up on the symbolism. For example, if you're working with pink, you might want to hold a pink rose or a pink heart.
- **Wear your color** – You can add it to your external wardrobe or keep it private (colored underwear, socks, something in your pocket). You can be deliberate about how you wear the color. For example, if you're working with red and want to feel more grounded, wear red socks!
- **Wear jewelry made of rocks or crystals** – You can combine the healing power of crystals with your Color Thinking work. You can select crystals for their properties, as well as their color.
- **Eat food that's your color—especially vegetables** – Chances are pretty good there is a nutrient in them that you crave, as well.

- **Give yourself a temporary tattoo** – Use a temporary tattoo pen to write your thoughts, belief, or a related affirmation somewhere on your body—like inside your wrist. Or use your color to draw a symbol that is meaningful to you. This works especially well for bridge thoughts!

- **Take time to make art, doodle, or do adult coloring** – Make sure your color is prominent. Experiment and see which other colors you want to combine with your color and check out their meaning. You might be getting a supporting message.

- **Notice what kinds of things pop up around you in your color** – You're already set up to notice your color. You'll probably be surprised how much it shows up, and in what ways. Is it in a piece of art? Objects? Signs? Decide this isn't *just coincidence*, but a signal of something to be gained in each instance. What does your intuition tell you? What can you learn from what you notice?

- **Put a scarf or piece of cloth over a lamp to create colored light** – (I don't need to say be careful not to create a fire hazard, do I?) Light colored candles. See if there's a scent you associate with your color (such as rose with pink, pine with green, cinnamon with red, jasmine with white, lavender with violet, to name a few). You can use the scent separately, like aromatherapy, or combine with candles of the same color. Some essential oil diffusers let you pick a color of light that goes with it. Get a colored night light.

- **Do color breathing** – Imagine your color in your mind's eye. Breathe in and visualize you're bringing the color into your body. On the exhale, breathe out the saturated, shadowy, negative aspects associated with your color—your old thoughts and beliefs.

On the inhale, breathe in the infused, positive aspects you crave—your new thoughts and beliefs. Double up on the woo woo by holding a crystal or lighting a candle.

- **Do some journaling** – Maybe this is something you already do. If that's the case, you're my hero! If you don't have a journaling habit, now could be a good time to adopt it—at least for a while. There are many kinds of journaling. I say, try them all. Try morning pages, thought downloads, storytelling, writing prompts. Answer questions, record color signs you're getting. Do artistic journaling. Do for anything else you might want to try. Definitely keep track of your thoughts, insights, signs, and progress.

Okay, those are a bunch of tools to put in your magic box. Believe it or not, that was just a few of the many possibilities. There are many more ways to incorporate your color into your support system. I'm sure you can come up with some ideas of your own. Pick the things that make sense to you and that you will actually do. For some specific tool ideas by color, go to the handy dandy resources in Chapter 14, or go to the website: **therainbowonion.com/bonus**.

Whatever you choose as your tools, I suggest you create a routine for yourself and do things on purpose. Set aside the time to move toward your destination and make it important. You might call this a habit, or you might call it a ritual. You choose.

How to Perform Quick Repairs

What do you do when the old belief shows up again? It will. This is a case of accepting the expected and being prepared. Just know you will probably get tired, you won't be hyper-vigilant 24/7, and you will find yourself slipping back into old thoughts and patterns or seeking out unhelpful evidence. Don't panic. It's totally normal. It's a sign of a healthy brain trying to take charge again. No biggie. Just get back on track. You can tell your brain *Thank you* or *Bless your heart* or *You sneaky bugger* and grab the steering wheel again (or tug on the leash, whichever metaphor you like best.) Make the thought correction you need to make and actively hunt down evidence to reinforce and reward your new thinking.

Then again, some totally unexpected shit might happen, and you might not be sure how to handle it. Hint: It's unexpected, so step one is to accept it. Don't resist it. That's too much work. Take charge. Think it through. Ask yourself helpful questions:

- What's the problem?
- How does this impact my new belief?
- Did this event trigger another old belief?
- What intentional thinking or thought corrections do I need to make?
- How am I using this situation as evidence?
- Is my confirmation bias or cognitive dissonance kicking in?
- Do I need to change my perspective?
- Are there any other powerful questions from Chapter 8 I can use?

In Case of Emergency, Break Glass and Square Breathe

If a situation causes you to feel like you're out of control, you might need a really quick pattern interrupt. I like square breathing. It's super easy, you don't need anything, and it's very effective. Here's how to do it:

- Stop whatever you're doing and sit still.
- Breathe in for four counts.
- Hold for four counts.
- Breathe out for four counts.
- Hold for four counts.
- Repeat four times (or more, if you need).

That's it. You'll feel calmer very quickly, and you should be able to get the survival brain out of the driver's seat without a bunch of wrestling. Square breathing is great to combine with color breathing, too, like we did back in Chapter 5 and earlier in this chapter.

Square breathing is effective at interrupting your usual stress patterns, because 1) you stop what you were doing, 2) you give your body a chance to metabolize the stress chemicals and bring your heart rate down, and 3) you make space to introduce a new, intentional behavior.

Once you have things back under *your* control, take a look around and do some investigating. What were the precursor emotions you were feeling immediately beforehand? What thoughts were you thinking? What position was your body in? Body language can reveal emotions we might not have noticed. Were there some subconscious triggers, like scents, sights, or muscle memory? When you have an idea of the causes of the stress pattern, you can go back and do something about it, as discussed above.

Preventative Maintenance

Finally, there are three things I'd like to make sure you add to your toolbox in the preventative maintenance category.

The first item is general self-care – The topic is *general*, but your toolbox contents are specific to you. What are the most effective elements of your self-care routine? The basics are things like eating right and getting plenty of rest, but you probably have some personal favorites. A few of mine are singing, petting furry animals, being among trees, and laughing. Pick yours and throw them into your toolbox and do them more frequently than you might normally.

The second item is movement – You need to move your body in some fashion to get the old stuff out. Move in any way that makes you breathe in and out more deeply than you do when you're just sitting and reading this. There's a whole big topic here—about the biology of belief, epigenetics, change, and transformation. It's a great topic, but too big for this book. For now, know that moving your body—especially outside in the fresh air and sunshine—is extremely effective for augmenting or supplementing all the other work you've got going here. It's just as magic as the other tools.

And finally, the third item is to find yourself some inspiration – Go out and actively look for it. Do things you might not ordinarily do, look in places you haven't looked in a while. Get out of your head and into the world. Look up, look around. Listen to someone else's story and wisdom. You can learn something from everyone. (Hey, learning about what you *don't* want is still learning!) Make time to be inspired—read, listen, look, watch, taste, touch, and smell. One of those. All of those.

I'm astounded sometimes at how little effort it takes to become inspired. Five minutes to open up my email and read the blog someone sent me, or pick a TED talk and listen. Or practice a little bibliomancy—isn't that a great word? It means to open up a book to a random page and just read for inspiration.

Every time I make the tiniest effort, I'm reminded of how nourishing inspiration can be. Why is it so easy for me to forget that? It'd be easy for me to find something wrong with me as an explanation for why I forget, but today I choose to believe I forget is so I can have the joy of rediscovery... Excuse me for a minute or two. I have to go turn this into a blog... Okay, I'm back.

Color Thinking Story – Some Items in People's Magic Boxes

Following are examples of some of the tools (support mechanisms) people put into their magical boxes (aka into their daily environments and routines) to remind them the most important thing they can do is monitor and manage their thinking. They leveraged their five senses to help them keep focus and to prop up their intentions.

Jordan's magic box was pink. He printed out his new belief as an affirmation and put it up all around the house while Zoe was on the trip with her mom. He associated roses with pink, so he got some roses and put them around the house. He also had a pink quartz crystal that he held sometimes, and he used a pink Aura-Soma pomander. Remember, he didn't have much pink in his everyday life, so when he used pink as a visual reminder, it really stuck out. A little pink went a long way!

Jenna's magic box was orange. She added orange to her wardrobe. She ate oranges and carrots, drank OJ, wrote "Nothing is too good to be true" in orange. She lit orange candles. She doodled with orange. She pulled out a citrine necklace. Jenna also focused on the second energy center (sometimes called a *chakra*), which is associated with orange. Jenna's work was all about healing the timeline, understanding she wasn't doomed to repeat some genetic curse. She also took off her *cursed* glasses and put on *orange* glasses. Jenna realized she needed a tool to help her see things differently.

Trina's magic box was red. Her affirmation was "I am inherently good and can trust myself. I choose the right tank at the right time," which she wrote in red and posted around. She wanted to be grounded in those thoughts, so she put a lot of things in her box! She wore red lipstick, red socks, and red underwear. There were walls in her home that were already red. She associated the scents of clove and frankincense with red, and just happened to have some doTERRA OnGuard essential oils! (There's more to Trina's red story coming up in Chapter 13.)

Color Thinking Exercise – Your Magic Box

Open your journal, or the worksheet and start listing and deciding on things to put in your own magic box. Here are some specific things you can do...

Your Color Support

Go to Chapter 14 and look up the Ideas for your color. Pick the Ideas that suit you or come up with your own. Write them down. Then list the things you'll need to do to get ready to do those ideas. Check them off as you do them, so you get that lovely task-satisfaction feeling, complete with happy brain hormones. Get whatever you need for support. Put things out where you can find them. Put up your visual reminders. Create your ritual. Put reminders in your calendar, if you need to.

Quick Repairs

What do you want for your "in case of emergency" plan?

What things do you want to have on hand to remind you of your new belief and thoughts if you fall back into old beliefs?

What questions do you need to have handy to be able to reframe a situation?

Your Preventative Maintenance Plan

What are you going to do for self-care?

What are you going to do for movement?

What are you going to do for inspiration?

Do. The. Things.

Cheeks down, butt in seat. The difference between someone who has done it and someone who hasn't is simply that: they've done it.

***

That's the whole Rainbow Onion Process! Those were all the steps.

You're ready now with your own magic. You've got what you need to change your thinking to something better on your journey to your goal.

If you want to look up more options, you can always check in on Part 3, coming up soon—the Reference Material section of the book.

For more hints on what to expect as you use *The Rainbow Onion* process, keep going to the next chapter.

CHAPTER 12

WHAT TO EXPECT

"When we see a vision for ourselves and decide to move toward it, we will immediately see mirrored back to us the ways we must adjust to align with that vision. This is not a sign that the decision is wrong, it is actually affirming that you are moving in the right direction and the new direction requires something new from you."

—Darla LeDoux

I chose this quote because I have been living in the world of signs for several months now. I had heard the idea that as soon as we make a decision, something will come up and challenge it, but I didn't understand why. If I had thought about it, I would have assumed the challenge was a confirmation step, as if the universe were sending us a message of *Are you sure you want to delete that?* or *Click to confirm your subscription.* Then I got an email from Darla LeDoux, who explained that these challenging signs are reminders that we need to make some adjustments if we're going to be in alignment with our new direction. Duh, right?

We spent some time last chapter preparing for the unexpected. Now let's spend some time preparing for the expected, too.

Here's a disclaimer—not everything in the lists below will happen for you. But some of them might, so that's enough reason for us to talk about them.

Signs, Signs, Everywhere a Sign

(Where did that earworm come from?) You *will* see signs everywhere. They'll come in a thousand different forms. Okay, maybe a couple of dozen.

You'll notice this strange paradox: You'll be spending more time inside your own head than normal, but you will also feel more connected to the world around you. That's because you're paying attention. That's mindfulness. That's why you'll begin to notice things, to see more signs. You'll recognize that signs are subtle, and it takes a little skill and a lot of practice to interpret them.

The most important thing to know is that you are the one who has to interpret your signs. *Interpreting signs* sounds so mystical, doesn't it? It doesn't have to be. You're simply finding the meaning in what surrounds you. You can use your heart and your mind and your intuition or the internet—all three?!—to discover what a sign means to you. You exploring and deciding on the meaning is the part that matters!

If you're the kind of person who's already comfortable asking for and receiving signs, your experience will only get deeper. It doesn't matter whether you ask God, angels, the universe, or any other entity in the multiverse.

If you don't have experience with signs, just be open and get ready, because they'll come anyway. You can chalk it up to coincidence (*mwahaha*), or synchronicity (*tee hee hee*). You can call them *God-winks*, or whatever you'd like.

Here are some of the probabilities for how you might experience signs:

- You'll notice your color waaaay more than you ever did before. Who knew it was so popular?
- You'll notice more written words about Your Thing, your beliefs, and the items in your magic box—articles, emails, books, posts, etc. Were people talking about this stuff all along and you just didn't know it?
- You'll notice more people talking about what you're thinking about, and not because you started the conversation. You'll just walk into them.
- You might notice a meaningful song pops up frequently around you, then gets stuck in your head.
- You'll be going along and suddenly feel like you need a sign that you're on the right track, and then BAM! something will appear that's a sign for you... as if just because you asked.
- You'll feel a gradual easing up of stress and tension, as your new beliefs become more and more believable. The cognitive dissonance *will* fade.

But before that happens, you'll probably encounter some challenging signs. Like, a problem comes up you didn't expect, or the exact opposite of what you want shows up, or someone tells you you're making a bad decision.

By the way, there are so many reasons people will butt in and give you their opinion on what you should do. Unless you've asked for their opinion, it's pretty likely the reason their giving has nothing to do with you and everything to do with their own story. You can totally decide that what they think of you is none of your business. As Anne Lamott says, "Help is the sunny side of control." Just sayin'.

But back to the challenging signs... You don't need to see them as evidence you're on the wrong track, even though your little ol' survival brain will try to tell you that. You can choose to recognize you're being presented with something YOU need to adjust, such as a thought correction or two.

The whole thing about signs is this: It's as if the universe is spying on you and then putting stuff in front of you—like Google or Facebook or whatever—only without the ads and waaay less creepy.

Just enjoy, and make meaning.

The Onion Things

In addition to signs and challenging things, there are some special things you can also expect. These are why The Rainbow Onion is an onion.

You can expect some intensity. This is because you're breaking through your outer shell. Have you ever noticed onions don't smell strong when they're just sitting there? They only give off that sharp, intense scent when you cut into them. When you cut into the defenses around your outdated beliefs, you can expect to find some intensity, pungency, and poignancy.

Some onions are stronger, hotter, more intense than others, which has to do with the sulfur content of the soil they grew in. Similarly, some of your beliefs are stronger and more intense than others, which has to do with how they were grown in you, in your internal soil. You might have picked a sweet, easy belief to update. Or you might have picked a hot and spicy belief. Remember, there is no one-size-fits-all approach to *The Rainbow Onion* process. You are absolutely unique. Just like everyone else is. Such a magnificent paradox that is!

There will be layers. As soon as you peel off the layer of an outer belief, you'll discover there's another one right below it. That's how this works. You can keep going to shift that next belief, or you can take a break and store the onion for a while!

Onions are widely used in cooking because they add so much flavor. Almost anything you cook becomes more flavorful, luscious, and savory when you add onions. Well, maybe not if you add onion to strawberry jam, but I have to admit I haven't tried it. Yet. In a similar way, as you open up to new thoughts and beliefs that serve you, you will undergo a profound transformation. As you become the boss of your life, you'll notice you aren't on autopilot as much. Your brain isn't defending you from quite so many preconceived dangers. You will experience more life. More of all the kinds of human experience, more of your life's flavors—the whole spectrum. Your emotions may become deeper and more complex. Your experiences become more flavorful. Your life becomes more savory.

Oh, I almost forgot—another special onion thing is there might be tears. You might sob, or ugly cry, or angry cry. Or maybe you just water up a bit. Your tears might be cleansing, purging, poignant, forgiving, burning—however they come to you, they are yours. Whatever happens, it's a good thing.

Color Thinking Story – Colors Can Be Signs, Too

You probably won't be at all surprised when I say colors can be gargantuan signs.

I was working with my coach, Mitch Matthews, talking through the very early stages of Color Thinking. I launched into my Aura-Soma background a bit—how I had been trained to use colors for healing and self-awareness, and then I started gushing about how colors are a language and how I like to use Color Thinking with my clients. He was intrigued, and said, "Tell me more." I randomly picked orange and started talking about how and why to use it in Color Thinking.

Mitch was floored because he had a current story about orange in his own life. He was getting a new vehicle and had recently felt led to get an orange Jeep. Like, seriously, *led*. Orange was already on his radar! So, why did I pick orange as an example when I was talking with him? Was it a coincidence? Oh, heck no. It wasn't random. It was a sign. It made Color Thinking personal for him, and it led us instantly to a discussion that was more meaningful than just about him getting a new vehicle. He told me what orange meant to him personally: Boldness, innovative thought, powerful warmth, and energy. I explained that orange often represents bliss, being in touch with deep intuition and healthy relationships, and a dramatic creative shift.

Being called to something orange, like a Jeep that he and his family would travel in all the time—was a super, literal message for him, it seemed to me: *take yourself and your family and drive towards bliss—with confidence*. It became even more meaningful when Mitch told me one of his favorite biblical verses is about being loved by God; the passage uses the Greek word *Perossis*, which means exceedingly, abundantly, beyond what you can imagine. We don't have a literal English translation for that type of love, but the closest word is *bliss*. Oh, and Mitch had already decided the license plate for his orange Jeep would refer to that verse. *Now* he knew why the Jeep was supposed to be orange.

Mitch was able to see the potential impact and power of Color Thinking quickly, maybe more quickly than I was, because the message of orange spoke to him in a deeply personal way. It wasn't only the coincidence of Mitch getting an orange Jeep and me mentioning the color orange. It was the depth and layers of meaning about orange that resonated with Mitch at a soul level.

That's an example of how color can be a powerful sign.

Color Thinking Exercise – Your Signs

Keep a journal (or use the journaling worksheets) to track signs for at least two weeks, maybe longer—however long you think you're still working on your new belief.

Make sure to track what you notice happening as you work through *The Rainbow Onion* process. It can be fun and a great help to have that info to look back on.

What signs do you encounter, and what do they mean to you? What are you noticing, feeling, learning as you go along? Do you think you might see another potential layer underneath the one you're been working on?

***

Now you've got some idea of what to expect as you move through the steps. This finishes up Part 2, *The Rainbow Onion* process.

The next section, Part 3, offers the Reference Materials. More tools for your magic box!

PART 3

REFERENCE MATERIALS

"There's always a strange feeling you get when you come across one particular line by chance. It feels somehow significant. That's irrational of course, but humans are irrational creatures."

—Mark Forsyth

This section of the book—Part 3—is like the reference section of the library. You probably don't go there looking for entertainment or a great read. You might not go there at all these days, because we can pretty much look up anything online. The readiness of the internet has trained us to go there to look up things whenever we need to know something specific. But since there isn't much on the internet (yet!) about Color Thinking, you'll need to rely on this reference section for now.

I've given you many metaphors to play with in this book. I understand things best when I have a simile, story, or metaphor. I hope there have been one or two that worked for you, whether *training your brain to sit* or *a childish soufflé* or *a glamping drama queen* or *a pilot grabbing the stick back from autopilot*, or *carts and horses*, or... Well, something's gotta stick, right?

The material in this chapter is included to give you more specific info to rely on as you go about updating your thoughts and beliefs. There are case studies showing examples of *The Rainbow Onion* process in action. There are lists offering specifics and details about color resources.

And, before we get to those, here's a story about the unexpected...

A Story of Layers

I told you to expect the unexpected, right? The unexpected is a big part of what happens when we start to peel back the layers. I don't mean that doing *The Rainbow Onion* work causes the unexpected to happen—not at all. The unexpected will always happen. It's part of life. But when you open yourself up to handle things differently, to drop your old beliefs, things will come up that might seem to be directly challenging your commitment, as I talked about in the last chapter. If you've built a good support system, you'll have the opportunity to process the unexpected things differently.

Let me give you an example.

While writing this book, when I reached this exact point in the manuscript, the unexpected happened. Then, while doing the revisions, something else unexpected happened.

Please know that while this may seem like a difficult story, there is also much beauty that comes through it.

The First Unexpected Thing

During the initial writing, I was right here when I got a phone call. I learned my brother Mark was dead, and he had committed suicide. It was not at all expected.

I stopped writing for a month and a half, then I come back to this place in the manuscript to resume writing again. I took a break because I didn't want to write this book while grieving. While I took the book break, I wrote other things, because I'm a writer.

I hoped I'd be inspired when I came back to writing the book. Although I am inspired to finish the book, and I am aware that I have grown during the break and learned tremendous things, I don't have any huge new insights—just an affirmation that I am "on the right track" and Color Thinking has many uses.

Unexpectedly, I feel good. Better, even. Grounded. My family got through that time with love for each other and for Mark. We definitely used color and light in our language. We were achingly, poignantly aware of all the signs around us, and we trusted them. We were patient. We made choices to be grace-full, grateful, loving, and kind. It's ironic to me that the world never seems so alive as when someone you love has died.

That experience and the timing of it really reinforced the onion metaphor for me—the intensity, tears, layers, and complexity. I couldn't go on writing and ignore the importance of this place in the book. I felt the need to *mark* this as a sacred place for me. Hmm. Mark this place with my brother Mark.

Now I can move on.

The Second Unexpected Thing

As I came back to the book to make revisions after getting feedback from my editor, I realized a second very unexpected thing had happened. Not only happened to me, but to the whole world.

At the time I'm writing this, I'm in lockdown to help prevent the spread of the Covid-19 virus. By the time you're reading this, things will be different. I don't know how things will look like for you, but I do know this unexpected event will have happened to you as well. It's happening to all of us around the world.

We are all now much more intensely aware of the beauty and interconnectedness and preciousness of life. We all have been reminded that there is a very full spectrum of experience and emotion in this thing that we call *life*. I know we will all have healing and processing and transforming to do as a result of our experiences. I know the only way we get through this is together. Tragedies and miracles will both be part of this story. How we tell the story, what we believe about ourselves, will shape who we are as a result of these unexpected events and how we move on.

Yes, things happen.

Prepare for the expected, expect the unexpected, experience and eventually accept them both. That, my friend, is truly life.

***

Okay, let's get back to what this section, Part 3, is about. I've already given you strategies and some stories. Maybe I've overloaded you with stories, strategies, and tools. You don't need to use everything, but I want you to have options!

Here are some more:

Chapter 13 – It's time for more stories, in the form of case histories. I've called these *case studies* because that sounds official. These are a few stories about how people have used Color Thinking and *The Rainbow Onion* process to reconcile their beliefs with their aspirations and transform themselves. Their journeys are far from complete. These case study stories are snapshots of a point in time. (You can find more stories on the website.)

Chapter 14 – Here's where detailed reference material lives. You can always check the website for more because I'll be continually adding and updating the resources there (it's a lot easier to include a video or an audio interview or inspirational color pictures on a website than in a book).

Chapter 15. Way back in the introduction, I told you there are additional ways to use Color Thinking - besides the full-fledged Rainbow Onion process, and I'd give you some examples. Here they are!

***

You can bookmark the resources listed here, to return to again and again as your journey through your own Rainbow Onion process. They're here for you!

CHAPTER 13

CASE STUDIES

"The human species thinks in metaphors and
learns through stories."

—Mary Catherine Bateson

You've had plenty of metaphors. Here are some more stories to help you pull the strategies and metaphors into the realm of real life.

Trina

Here's the update on Trina I promised. It turns out she was pretty in touch with her intuition and picked red for a very good reason. Remember she felt exhausted and drained as if her energy was flowing from the wrong tank? Well, she was completely right. Her exhaustion stemmed from doing too much and not taking care of herself. It turned out she was also bleeding internally and didn't consciously know it. She really was in survival mode, because she was slowly bleeding to death! Trina finally went to the ER, was diagnosed, was scheduled for surgery, and had several blood transfusions. She had been pushing through an ankle injury, taking NSAIDs, traveling a lot, and was highly stressed. She really needed some red! And, yes, she did recover.

Reina

Reina had been studying and testing for her complex certification in a particular field of accounting for several years. She would take one part of her exams and pass them, then move on to study for the next one, only to have the credits for the first exam expire before she'd finished the whole process. Or she would take a test and not pass it in time. She couldn't see a good reason for what was happening. She was certainly smart enough and competent enough to get the certification. She studied long and hard. She was a capable businesswoman. She had all the traits, education, and qualifications she needed to succeed—she just couldn't seem to get through the exam sequence.

Reina began to doubt her ability to get it done. She felt overwhelmed. There was a bit of self-pity as well, along with a growing lack of focus. What was the point in all of that work if she was ever going to pass?

Reina decided to work with the color magenta. She needed to focus, and she needed to pay attention to the details. She wanted confidence. She wanted to finish the certification with grace and gratitude, and to still love what she was doing in her work.

Her mantra became *love is in the little things*. She remembered that her grandmother had lived that way, and she could feel her grandmother's love when she thought about it. She decided to use magenta to remind her to change her attitude about how she studied and how she took the tests. By focusing on the little things—the details of the process—she moved out of overwhelm. She started passing the tests the first time, with high scores.

Within a year Reina finished all the requirements and became certified, and now she has a growing practice. Most importantly, she was able to keep reminding herself that she was doing the certification because she loved the work, and she was more than capable.

Deirdre

Deirdre was a client who came to me saying she wasn't really in happy with where her career seemed to be going, how much time it took out of her life, and how little time and energy she had left for anything else.

She worked in a male-dominated industry and was the only woman in her role in her organization. She didn't see anyone who looked like her in any leadership roles in her department. She didn't have any examples, mentors, or support to help her develop her own style of leadership or deal with the struggles she had on a daily basis.

Deirdre was jealous of how "easy" the men had it compared to her situation. Her work/life relationship felt completely out of balance. She couldn't get a handle on her to-do list—it was out of control, and she felt like every day was filled with conflict and conflicting priorities. She felt trapped. She thought about making a job or career change but couldn't see any viable options.

Deirdre didn't take the time to take care of herself. She worked six days a week, from dawn to beyond dusk. She had no hobbies or activities outside work besides life chores. She didn't have time for travel or her family. She didn't make time to exercise or eat well. That way of living began to show up in severe and scary health issues.

Deirdre chose to work with green. She craved balance. She wanted to be able to see the big picture. She wanted to feel like she had options. She wanted expansiveness.

One of the ways Deirdre worked with green was to tease out the thoughts behind her feelings of jealousy. She was jealous of the men she worked with because she thought they had it easy in ways she believed she'd never be able to have.

For example, Deirdre believed she'd never be able to be herself without worrying about whether her boss was uncomfortable with her style of communicating, was holding her to a different standard because she was a woman, or was judging her as too emotional. She constantly felt she needed to prove herself.

I want to be clear here. The work world is full of places where women are held to a different performance standard, where we are judged for having different leadership or communication styles, and where stereotypes, biases, and prejudice abound, especially in STEM (science, technology, engineering, and mathematics). That's just reality at this time. That needs to change, but it won't change overnight.

Deirdre's health couldn't wait for external things to change. Deirdre was not wrong about her work environment, but she felt jealous and trapped because *she believed* she would never be able to stop worrying about how her boss reacted or whether she measured up. It was the worry that trapped her.

We played a lot with *so what?* So what if Deirdre's boss was uncomfortable? So what if he didn't always agree with her or understand her reactions? So what if her responses were different from other people's? So what if her co-workers had it easier? So what if she didn't get everything on her to-do list done? So what if she did a shitty job? So what if she got fired? (She didn't, but we needed to push the envelope.) We also looked at other questions. What was most important to her? What were her true priorities? We didn't only list her priorities, we ranked them.

When Deirdre was able to see that her health and her family were higher on the list than her career, she realized she hadn't been making choices based on HER priorities. She'd been letting the choices make her. When she realized that, she wanted to take responsibility back into her own hands.

Deirdre was fortunate enough to be in a rural place where she was surrounded by green—fields, crops, orchards. As she made time to walk in expansive vistas of green, she could feel things opening up. She began to believe she did have options, and she took the initiative to explore them.

She made some difficult choices. She prioritized her life and her health. She chose to accept a different job with a significantly lower level of stress. She believes she will be able to be much more comfortable being herself in the new role, while also balancing the important things in her life. She IS being successful—because she believes in herself.

***

The stories below focus more on "before" situations, and the colors people chose to work with, and why.

Tim

Tim was ready for a job or career change. He had put in years climbing the corporate ladder and he was traveling way too much. His days were all work, and he had no time for life!

He figured he had about fifteen more years before he would want to retire, and he wanted to spend those fifteen years having a blissful, balanced life—doing work he loved while having enough time and energy to live a life he loved, too. He wanted to find his bliss, so he chose to work with orange.

Joni

Joni had just found out her sister had terminal cancer. They didn't know how much time she had but knew it was likely only months. Joni experienced grief in advance. She knew she wanted to be deeply present with her sister for the time they did have. She wanted to prepare for her sister's transition and take loving care of own self as well, before, during, and after.

Joni knew she wanted to work with violet. She needed support and reminders and the occasional question to help her focus on what was important for her in the moment.

Joni navigated her loss with a grace I've rarely seen. Her loving kindness was an inspiration to me, and she taught me much about violet and transformation.

Nicky

Nicky was a successful mom, career woman, and member of her community. She was confident, informed, decisive, adventurous, sympathetic, and empathetic. Right up until she wasn't.

When Nicky started doing *The Rainbow Onion* process, she said she felt overwhelmed. She couldn't make decisions. She felt stuck in analysis paralysis and didn't trust her own judgment. She agonized over every decision, trying to take everyone into consideration and make everyone happy, but she was also tired of reacting to everyone else's emotions and attitudes.

Nicky described herself as flooded with guilt, anger, and fear. She wasn't living a life she chose, because she wasn't capable of making choices. She felt petrified of the consequences of her decisions.

When Nicky really narrowed down her story, she realized her gem was *I'm afraid to make a decision.*

Nicky did make a choice, one that led to more action, bravery, and joy. She chose to work with yellow.

Laura

When Laura told me her story, she said she grew up in a family that didn't really express emotions. She was the youngest, a "surprise" baby, and her siblings were all much older. Laura was a child among her young adult siblings. She was always told how to behave, to settle down, to act more like her siblings. She was told her emotions were "too big," and she believed it. She spent years feeling uncomfortable sharing her true thoughts, feelings, and points of view. She throttled down, suppressed herself to keep peace and calm in the family. Laura turned to writing for relief, which worked for a while.

As time went on, the family continued to compare where Laura was in her life with where the rest of the siblings were. Because she was so much younger, that wasn't a fair comparison (as if comparing is ever a good idea). The family mythology about Laura was that she was irresponsible, not good with money, couldn't be trusted to make big decisions, etc. Laura bought into that, too.

When Laura and her siblings had to deal with aging and ailing parents, it brought everything to the forefront for her. She wanted to have a voice in the decisions being made. She wanted her siblings to include and respect her. She wanted to have conversations that included emotions.

Laura felt misunderstood and frustrated. She told me she had no voice. She wanted to write—because writing had always worked in the past, but it just wasn't coming. She wanted better communication with her family but felt unheard. She wanted to be able to speak her mind and her heart.

Laura considered working with turquoise (which can help with learning to communicate the feelings side of things) but chose to work with blue. She followed her intuition to decide between the two. Part of what helped her decide was knowing she also wanted to activate her throat chakra and her voice, since the throat chakra is associated with the color blue. Laura chose to concentrate on finding her voice and being heard, which is why she ultimately chose blue.

By the way, when Laura picked colorful blue things as her support, they often had a hint of turquoise in them! The next layer she worked with was, in fact, turquoise. Because there's always another layer.

***

Now it's your turn! Dig into the lists in the next chapter to move into your own story.

CHAPTER 14

COLOR DETAILS

"Time spent with cats is never wasted."

—Sigmund Freud

I chose the quote above because I can. It's my book. That quote has been on a refrigerator magnet at my house for so long I can't remember where the magnet came from. I happen to think the quote is true, but I'm sure there are some who read it and disagree. Some may vehemently disagree. Some might be allergic to cats.

Interpreting the language of color works a bit like that—not everyone will agree, and the "right" interpretations are personal. In this chapter, I offer resources and references. However, even though I'm pretty much an expert on this stuff, I'm not an expert on *you*. You are. You, ultimately, have the final say about what a color means to you, which questions speak to you, how you want to use color, etc. You get to pick what goes in YOUR book. (Just don't dye your cat magenta if you're working with magenta.)

Below are Current State descriptors listed by color. These are the shadow-side descriptors for each color. When you're looking for a color to help you move through *The Rainbow Onion* process, look through these to find the Current State that most closely fits for you. The summary statements can help you narrow down your search or decide between colors. You can also confirm your choice of a color to help you by considering what you crave and looking for the opposite in this list.

When in doubt, choose deep magenta. Really. Deep magenta is a general, all-purpose color for this work because it contains all the other colors within it. It's like aspirin—you don't have to tell aspirin where to work in your body; it just knows. Deep magenta works the same way in this Rainbow Onion process.

Current State Descriptors

Color	Current State	Summary
Red	angry, resentful, threatened, survival mode, lots of drama and/or microdrama, unsafe, not grounded, orphaned, greedy, materialistic, hoarding, not enough energy or passion, weak, frail, waning life force	No power or safety
Pink	unloved, hurt, needy or clingy, smothered or smothering, self-loathing, too vulnerable, not accepted or acceptable, uncared for or uncaring, conditional love	No love or self-confidence
Coral	alone, lonely, no community, broken, unsupported, don't fit in, out on the edge, unequal relationships	No tribe or support
Orange	trauma, history keeps repeating, defined by family history, trapped by fate and/or	No choice; scarcity

	genetics, cursed, no bliss, unhealthy relationships, co-dependent	
Gold	self-doubt, irrational fear, mistrust, uneducated, *I never learn*, fear of being able to handle the unknown	No wisdom or confidence
Yellow	fear, worry, confusion, anxiety, unsafe, analysis paralysis from fear, "rational" fear, no joy, pessimistic, negative	No joy or optimism
Olive	guilt, bitter, persecuted, judged, shame, unable to lead, defensive, cut off from feminine traits, don't trust intuition, hopeless	No support or hope
Green	trapped, constrained, jealousy, envy, out of balance, indecisive, too much conflict, can't find truth, no growth	No options or balance
Turquoise	follower, too serious, not creative, torn between two viewpoints, dithering, hyperactive without direction	No certainty or sense of self
Blue	lost, sad, distant, unheard, no voice, no say, no peace, no sense of direction, poor communications, misunderstood, hold your tongue	No voice or peace
Royal Blue	scattered, isolated, untethered, wackadoodle, too sensitive, flighty, out of	No intuition or faith

	touch, no spiritual connection, don't trust own intuition	
Violet	spacey, in transition, stuck in grief, over-thinking, caught up in analysis, unfocused, can't move on	No movement or direction
Magenta	self-pity, uncaring, smothered, overwhelmed, ungrateful, can't focus or plan, too many details	No perspective or grace
Deep Magenta	quicksand, weighed down, amorphous, *missed my potential*, too late, out of touch with Source, can't make progress, (for general, all-purpose color aid)	No time or progress
Clear	suffering, pent-up tears, darkness, pessimistic, murky	No clarity or light
White	overly responsible, unclean, contaminated, heavy burden, unsupported, can't hear the messages or see the signs	No innocence

When you've chosen your color from the list above, you look up the other resources for that color in the list below, which is organized by color.

This list is only a sampling because the possibilities are quite plentiful. There's a plethora of possibilities, really. You can absolutely feel free to mix and match colors and meaning, as works for you, as I've said at least seven times already in this book, if not a million. There are more resources about individual colors on the website (**therainbowonion.com/bonus**), because I can update that whenever we discover something new.

Oh, a note about picking your questions from the Sample Questions lists below: You don't have to answer every question when you're working through The Rainbow Process with a particular color. Look for the few questions with the power to change your perspective and upset your thinking (imagine apples spilling out of a basket and bouncing all over the floor of your mind!). If a question makes you really think or causes a strong reaction—even if it's denial—take some time with that question. Make it personal by changing up the wording to fit your exact situation. If none of the questions fits exactly, check out the list of general questions at the end. You can find lots of additional questions on the website, in a section of questions arranged by topic (in addition to the lists of questions arranged by color).

Not every color below has obvious choices for each of the categories. For example, not every color has an energy center or chakra it's associated with. Not every color has a flower or food. Your choice of fragrance might be different than what I've suggested.

These are not rules! They are meant to be inspiration. In any and every case, choose what feels right to you. Have fun with it!

Resources by Color

Red

What I Crave (Future State)

- safety
- security

- comfort

- energy

- passion

- power

- trust in home

- sanctuary

- groundedness

- foundations

- courage

- strength

Sample *I am* / Gem Statements

- I don't feel safe.

- I have no power.

- I'm always in survival mode.

- Everything feels like a crisis.

- I don't have a foundation.

- I have no energy.

Sample Questions

- What would make me feel safe?

- What would make me feel grounded?

- What would I do if I weren't in survival mode?

- What if there is no crisis?

- What if this is how things are supposed to be?

- Where do I get my energy?

- What if I had enough energy?

- Where do I get my strength?

- How can I get the energy/strength/courage I need?

- What is my sanctuary?

- What do I need for my foundation?

- How am I strong?

- How can I parent myself?

- How can I give myself what I need?

- How has this served me in the past?

- What if this were no longer true for me?

- How is this limiting me?

- Who would I be if I had the energy/passion I want?

- What if I am already safe?

- How can I put down roots?

- Do I know my roots?

Sample Mantras or Beliefs

- I am safe.

- I have everything I need right now.

- My home is my sanctuary.

- I have all the strength I need.

Ideas for Using Red

- Food: Beet, cherry, strawberry, raspberry, pomegranate, chard, red pepper, tomato, cranberry, watermelon, hibiscus tea

- Flowers: Red rose, tulip, hibiscus

- Spices: Chili, cinnamon,

- Scents: Cinnamon, clove, cherry, frankincense

- Crystals and Stones: Ruby, garnet, red agate, carnelian
- Energy Center: 1 / root chakra
- Clothing: Red socks, shoes, underwear

Pink

What I Crave (Future State)

- acceptance
- being loved and loving
- self-love
- forgiveness
- self-confidence
- trust
- being enough
- deserving to be here

Sample *I am* / Gem Statements

- I am unloved.
- I am unworthy of love.
- I hate myself.
- I can't forgive myself.
- I smother everyone.

Sample Questions

- What thoughts would be more accepting and compassionate?
- How can I look at this situation in a way that's less judgmental and more supportive?

- What can I think and believe that will make me feel less critical of myself (or someone else)?
- What would unconditional love do in this situation? How can I be that love?
- Where have I witnessed unconditional love?
- What if I am worthy?
- How can I be kind?
- What if I am enough?
- What if I love myself?
- How has this situation served me?
- How have I used this as an excuse?
- What am I making this mean about me?
- What if it isn't about me at all?

Sample Mantras or Beliefs

- I trust that I am loved.
- I am enough.
- I deserve to be here.
- I love and forgive myself.
- Other people have reasons for what they do that have nothing to do with me.
- I am generous and loving.
- I give myself what every human needs.

Ideas for Using Pink

- Food: Rhubarb, pink grapefruit, pink lemonade,
- Flowers: Pink rose, chrysanthemum, camellia, geranium

- Spices: Himalayan pink salt, pink pepper

- Scents: Rose, almond blossom, carnation

- Crystals and Stones: Rose quartz, pink tourmaline, pink opal,

- Energy Center: Heart

- Clothing: Top, scarf, tie

Coral

What I Crave (Future State)

- community

- belonging to a tribe

- being able to give and to receive

- supported

- understanding the wisdom of love

- mutual support

Sample *I am* / Gem Statements

- I am alone.

- I have no tribe.

- I never fit in.

- I feel broken.

- My relationships are never equal.

Sample Questions

- Who do I want my tribe to be?

- How can I be a better member of a tribe?

- Who is my community?

- What can I give to my community?

- What do I need from my community?
- What if I can make my own community?
- Where can I find my community?
- What does an equal relationship really look like?
- How can I be more supportive?
- Do I have my own back?
- What if I chose to live on the edge?
- How can I help myself heal?
- How has being alone served me?
- Can I be alone without being lonely?

Sample Mantras or Beliefs

- I am a vital member of my community.
- I choose my tribe and they choose me.
- I am completely supported.
- I have my own back.

Ideas for Using Coral:

- Food: Salmon, ruby red grapefruit, cantaloupe, peach smoothie
- Flowers: Gladiolus, canna, gerbera daisy,
- Spices: Caribbean spice, Himalayan salt
- Scents: Beach, grapefruit,
- Crystals and Stones: Costume coral (rather than real coral), morganite
- Energy Center: Heart, sacral chakra
- Clothing: Top, scarf, tie

Orange

What I Crave (Future State)

- healing of the past

- bliss

- abundance

- understanding of abundance

- radically different thinking

- imagination

- freedom from family trauma

Sample *I am* / Gem Statements

- I am cursed.

- I'm doomed by genetics.

- I'm stuck in a loop.

- I'm a victim of trauma

- My relationships are codependent.

Sample Questions

- What if there's nothing that's too good to be true?

- What can I think that is radically different?

- What do I have in abundance?

- What can I give or do that would be too good to be true?

- What would I heal in the past if I could?

- What can I send forward in time to my future self?

- What can I send backward in time to my past self?

- Who would I be if I weren't cursed?

- Who will I be when I am blessed?

- How am I letting this define me? Why?
- How has being this way served me in the past?
- Does this serve me now?
- What if I'm using this as an excuse (to live small, avoid taking responsibility, avoid risk, avoid an emotion)?
- How am I using this as an excuse?
- What do I need to learn in order to move on?
- What evidence do I have that I am not my genetics?
- What beliefs did I inherit rather than choose?
- What if I have exactly enough? What if I have more than enough?
- What is my bliss?

Sample Mantras or Beliefs

- Nothing is too good to be true.
- I am not defined by my past.
- I am not a victim.
- I am in charge of my life and I take charge starting now.
- I have more than enough.
- I deserve to be happy.
- I know what brings me bliss.

Ideas for Using Orange

- Food: Orange, carrot, sweet potato, pumpkin, pepper, mango
- Flowers: Poppy, begonia, canna, gerbera daisy, marigold
- Spices: Pumpkin spice blend, citrus,
- Scents: Orange, tangerine, peach,
- Crystals and Stones: Topaz, citrine, tourmaline

- Energy Center: 2 / sacral chakra
- Clothing: Skirt, pants, shorts, scarf

Gold

What I Crave (Future State)

- wisdom
- confidence in abilities
- deep knowing
- ability to look for new evidence
- insightfulness
- commitment
- follow-through

Sample *I am* / Gem Statements

- I doubt myself all the time.
- I can't trust myself.
- I never learn.
- I'm afraid of what I don't know.
- I have lots of phobias.

Sample Questions

- What do I really, really know?
- Where does my wisdom live?
- What has my life taught me?
- What did I come here knowing?
- How do I learn best?
- What am I afraid to know?

- How can I accept the unknown without being afraid?

- What if I'm afraid but I know things anyway?

- What do I trust? How? Why?

- What evidence do I have now that proves that I do know?

- What if I didn't doubt myself?

- What are my insights?

- What are my real gifts?

- What am I making my self-doubt mean?

- What evidence do I have that I have been wise?

Sample Mantras or Beliefs

- I trust my own inner wisdom.

- I know my gifts, abilities, and contributions.

- I live and learn, in spite of fear.

- My wisdom guides me through the unknown.

Ideas for Using Gold

- Food: Pepper, banana, golden beet, pasta, chard, pineapple

- Flowers: Dahlia, sunflower, poppy,

- Spices: Turmeric, ginger, saffron

- Scents: Orange, tangerine, vanilla

- Crystals and Stones: Gold, tiger eye, goldstone glass

- Energy Center: Seed star center

- Clothing: Jewelry, hat, scarf, belt, glitter

Yellow

What I Crave (Future State)

- joy
- optimism
- bravery / courage
- taking action in spite of fear
- freedom from worry and anxiety
- laughter

Sample *I am* / Gem Statements

- I'm always afraid.
- I worry constantly.
- I have so much anxiety.
- I'm afraid to make decisions.
- I have no joy.

Sample Questions

- What do I fear?
- What brings me joy?
- How are fear and joy related?
- Am I thinking a certain way because I'm afraid?
- How can I change the way I think?
- What is the worst that can happen?
- What if I chose optimism or joy?
- What if I decide fear won't stop me?
- How can I be brave?
- What if joy is contagious?

- How can I make a decision anyway?
- What am I making my fear mean about me?
- Where can I find more joy?
- How can I make more joy?
- How can I laugh more?
- What really makes me happy?
- How am I already brave?
- What evidence do I have that I have been brave?
- What life do I choose?
- How can I add adventure?

Sample Mantras or Beliefs

- My joy is my strength.
- I am braver than I knew.
- Anxiety is just an emotion.
- Worry pretends to be useful.
- I am making the best decisions for me right now.
- I choose to live my life _____.

Ideas for Using Yellow:

- Food: Banana, lemon, egg, pepper, corn, apple, pineapple
- Flowers: Marigold, daisy, sunflower, rose
- Spices: Curry, mustard, turmeric
- Scents: Lemon, pineapple, banana
- Crystals and Stones: Amber, citrine, calcite
- Energy Center: 3 / solar plexus
- Clothing: Worn anywhere

Olive

What I Crave (Future State)

- hope
- freedom from guilt and shame
- being cured of bitterness
- feminine style of leadership
- loving intuition
- being unjudged and judgment-free
- generosity and nurturing
- not being reactionary

Sample *I am* / Gem Statements

- I am full of guilt and shame.
- I don't trust my intuition.
- I feel hopeless.
- I am so defensive.
- Everyone is against me.

Sample Questions

- What if I chose not to feel guilt or shame again?
- What have I really done to be so guilty about?
- How can I choose not to be as defensive?
- What *shoulds* are controlling my life?
- What *shoulds* am I willing to throw away?
- What if I were never judged again?
- What if I never judged anyone else again?

- What judgments about other people are actually about me judging myself?
- What if I choose to be a different kind of leader?
- What if I lead with love and trust?
- How can I use my intuition to become free from shame and judgment?
- What if I'm not being persecuted?
- How can I let go of this bitterness?
- How can I feel more alive?
- What do I make this guilt and shame mean?
- What new evidence can I see?
- How can I see the other side?

Sample Mantras or Beliefs

- I am freed of the burdens of guilt and shame.
- There are no *shoulds* in my life. I make my own choices.
- I let go of bitterness.
- I am neither judging nor judged.
- I choose to lead by love and example.

Ideas for Using Olive

- Food: Green olive, artichoke, asparagus,
- Plant/Flowers: Fern, olive branch; any type of plants
- Spices: Rosemary, thyme
- Scents: Sweet olive oil, bergamot
- Crystals and Stones: Jade, malachite, moldavite, agate
- Energy Center: Heart chakra, solar plexus chakra

- Clothing: Any

Green

What I Crave (Future State)

- expansiveness
- seeing the big picture
- lots of options and choices
- balance
- loving openness
- resolution of conflicts
- growth

Sample *I am* / Gem Statements

- I feel trapped.
- I am so jealous.
- I'm surrounded by conflict.
- I can't find a way out.
- I don't have any options.

Sample Questions

- What do I believe I can't have?
- What if I *can* have that?
- How can I see the bigger picture?
- What if I do have options? What might they be?
- If I step back, what do I see?
- What is really important to me?
- What would bring me into balance?

- What if the options really are expansive?

- In the big picture, what do I really want?

- What if all the constraints fell away?

- How am I making myself feel trapped?

- How am I letting this situation define me and my options?

- How am I using this situation to hide?

- How does being jealous benefit me?

Sample Mantras or Beliefs

- I have so many options!

- I am not jealous of anyone. I can have good things, too.

- My world is expansive.

- I can choose balance in my life

- I am in charge of my life.

- I am not trapped.

Ideas for Using Green

- Food: Chard, kale, broccoli, pea, avocado, green apple, kiwi, pepper, brussels sprout, green tea, lime, mint

- Flowers: Green lily, zinnia, carnation, shamrock, fern, grass

- Herbs and Spices: Dill, parsley, basil

- Scents: Grass, tea, juniper, lime, pine, mint, bamboo

- Crystals and Stones: Emerald, tourmaline, chrysoprase, peridot

- Energy Center: 4 / heart chakra

- Clothing: Upper body – shirt, coat, wrap, scarf, necklace, pendant

Turquoise

What I Crave (Future State)

- creativity
- individuality
- finding my way
- playfulness
- ability to communicate emotions
- blending to find balance, especially heart and head

Sample *I am* / Gem Statements

- I waver between my head and heart.
- I'm torn between x and y.
- I run around like a chicken with my head cut off.
- I'm not creative.
- I'm such a follower.

Sample Questions

- What if it isn't either/or?
- How can I blend and balance instead of choose either/or?
- What if my head and my heart are *both* right?
- How can I find a creative solution?
- What is MY truth here?
- What can I blend to come up with options?
- What if there is no *should*?
- What if I'm unique, and it's all about doing things my way?
- How can I be creative anytime I want?
- What do I get out of dithering?

- How can I make my creativity bigger?
- How can I share what I do?

Sample Mantras or Beliefs

- I know how to use both my heart and my head.
- There is always an answer that includes both love and logic.
- I am so creative!
- I have my own way of doing things that works well for me.
- I know who I am.

Ideas for Using Turquoise

- Food, Flowers, Spices, Scents: Natural turquoise items in these categories are rare, so consider serving food on turquoise plates, drinking out of a turquoise mug or glass, using a turquoise flower vase, etc. This is perfect for turquoise because it requires you to be creative. Lovingly select what you want to use!
- Scents: Beach, seafoam, tropical
- Crystals and Stones: Turquoise, aventurine, opalite
- Energy Center: High heart
- Clothing: Upper body, high heart; scarf, vest, wrap, necklace

Blue

What I Crave (Future State)

- meaning
- purpose
- direction
- seeing potential outcomes

- peace
- ease
- coming to terms with sadness
- finding my voice
- being heard and understood

Sample *I am* / Gem Statements

- I feel so sad.
- I'm lost.
- I don't know my purpose.
- No one understands me.
- I have no voice.

Sample Questions

- What if I did know my purpose?
- What medium of expression might I use for my voice?
- How can I be at peace with my point of view?
- What would I say if I could?
- How can I move through sadness?
- What if people did understand me?
- How can I be heard?
- Do I listen to and understand myself?
- What do I most want people to understand about me?
- Who do I really want to understand me?
- What would I like my purpose to be?
- What if I could express my emotions in words?
- How has being sad served me?

- If I weren't lost, where would I be?

- If I weren't lost, what would I be?

- What keeps me from feeling at peace?

- What do I need in order to resolve my inner conflict?

- What if something else is more important than conflict?

Sample Mantras or Beliefs

- I am discovering and defining my purpose.

- My path is getting clearer and clearer.

- I have found my voice.

- I experience more and more peace and ease.

- I understand and am understood.

Ideas for Using Blue

- Food: Blueberry, blue corn, blue potato, plum, blue tea

- Flowers: Hydrangea, delphinium, grape hyacinth, bluebell, sweet pea

- Spices: (Hard to find); fruit and berry extracts

- Scents: Peppermint, eucalyptus, sea, salt

- Crystals and Stones: Sapphire, lapis lazuli, aquamarine, fluorite

- Energy Center: 5 / throat chakra

- Clothing: Scarf, turtleneck, hoody, buff, cowl

Royal Blue

What I Crave (Future State)

- intuition

- faith

- being in touch with spirit and spirituality
- access to higher mind and gifts
- higher purpose
- belief systems

Sample *I am* / Gem Statements

- I'm too sensitive.
- People think I'm an airhead.
- I'm out of touch with my spirituality.
- I feel really scattered.
- I don't know what I believe.

Sample Questions

- What is my source?
- What do I really believe?
- What is my spirituality?
- What sustains me?
- How am I connected?
- How can I be tethered?
- How has my intuition served me in the past?
- When have I trusted or not trusted my intuition?
- When did I lose touch?
- What if I'm not too sensitive? What else could this be about?
- How am I not alone?
- What if I'm causing my isolation?
- What does being scattered give me?
- What do I need in order to be more focused?

- What if I had faith?

- How can I grow my spiritual connection?

- What am I making this all mean about me?

- What is spirit?

Sample Mantras or Beliefs

- I have faith in myself and my spirituality.

- All is good and well with the world.

- I am exactly where I am supposed to be.

- There is a higher purpose in everything.

- I am growing my intuition and gifts.

Ideas for Using Royal Blue

- Food: Concord grape, plum, purple potato

- Flowers: Iris, periwinkle, agapanthus

- Spices: (Hard to find); fruit, berry, and lavender extracts

- Scents: French lavender, incense

- Crystals and Stones: Sapphire, kyanite, lapis lazuli, sodalite

- Energy Center: 6 / third eye chakra

- Clothing: Hats, scarf, hair decoration, jewelry

Violet

What I Crave (Future State)

- transformation

- healing

- growth

- ability to transition and/or able to move on

- purposeful movement

- transitions

- purposeful alchemy

- devotion

Sample *I am* / Gem Statements

- I can't get over my grief.

- I overthink everything.

- I can't focus.

- I can't move on to what's next.

- I'm always in transition.

Sample Questions

- What in my life is calling for transformation?

- How am I stuck?

- What if I weren't stuck?

- Who do I want to be next?

- What kind of alchemy do I want in my life?

- What will I be when I transform?

- How am I in the process of metamorphosis?

- What is transcendence for me?

- What are some purposeful steps I can take to move forward?

- What kind of devotion can I add?

- What if I could move on?

- Who will I be in my next phase?

- Who am I growing into?

- What evidence do I have of healing happening in my life?

- Who in my life is in their own transition? How do I want to handle that?
- What is my next best move?
- What if I just trust this transition?
- What do I need to let go of?
- How can I think differently about death?

Sample Mantras or Beliefs

- I am becoming who I am meant to be.
- I am moving into the next stage of my life.
- I carry my loved one in my heart.
- I am moving through my grief with love and patience.
- It is normal to experience transitions.
- My transformation is astounding!
- I am protected by violet light that transforms everything into good.

Ideas for Using Violet:

- Food: Grape, purple potato, eggplant, red cabbage, blackberry, fig, raisin, purple carrot
- Flowers: Violet, lavender
- Spices: Lavender, thyme, grape
- Scents: Lavender, grape, lilac, violet
- Crystals and Stones: Amethyst, fluorite,
- Energy Center: 7 / crown chakra
- Clothing: Worn anywhere

Magenta

What I Crave (Future State)

- expressing love through action
- working through the details
- gratitude
- grace
- caring
- finding love in the little things
- small, persistent actions

Sample *I am* / Gem Statements

- I'm stuck in self-pity.
- I don't care about other people's stuff.
- I feel overwhelmed.
- I can't make a plan
- I'm smothered in details.

Sample Questions

- What is one detail I can really see?
- What is one small thing that I can do right now?
- Where is the grace in this?
- How can I be graceful?
- What am I grateful for?
- What do I care most about?
- How can I show that I care?
- What can I do for someone else today?
- What if I can make one small decision?

- What if I think small?
- What if I weren't overwhelmed?
- What one small thing would make a difference?
- What details have I been missing?
- Where is the little love?
- What is in the way of me seeing the details?
- How can I make my focus/world smaller for now?
- So what if I lose sight of the big picture for a while?

Sample Mantras or Beliefs

- I express my love in the details.
- I am full of grace and gratitude.
- I make progress one little step at a time.
- I am a perseverance machine!
- I can handle anything—one step, one day at a time!

Ideas for Using Magenta

- Food: Raspberry, red cabbage, dragon fruit, radish, red potato
- Flowers: Bougainvillea, rhododendron, geranium, aster, cosmos
- Spices: Delicate flavors of your choice
- Scents: Raspberry, delicate and faint fragrances
- Crystals and Stones: Tourmaline, pale amethyst, dyed agate, rose quartz
- Energy Center: 8 / soul Star
- Clothing: Anything

Deep Magenta

What I Crave (Future State)

- big shift

- manifestation

- recognition of potential

- reprioritization

- re-centering

- pulling out of the muck

- dumping the drama

- taking big actions

Sample *I am* / Gem Statements

- I am so stuck (bogged down).

- I feel weighed down.

- It's always too late.

- I'm too old.

- Nothing is clear.

Sample Questions

- What could be perfect about being stuck right now?

- What if it isn't too late?

- What if now is exactly the right time?

- What if there were a way to get a do-over?

- Where do I crave clarity the most?

- What does all this drama give me?

- Who would I be without the drama?

- What if I were a person who took big action?

- What one thing could I do that would make the biggest impact?
- What one type of progress would change everything? How would it change?
- What are my top priorities right now?
- What do I most want to manifest? Do I believe that is possible? What evidence do I have or need that it's here?
- What do I want to release?
- What would I pack into a hot air balloon to send up and away?

Sample Mantras or Beliefs

- I know my own priorities.
- I am the one who takes action.
- My future is up to me.
- I'm experiencing a huge shift in my life.
- I am manifesting today's dreams now.

Ideas for Using Deep Magenta

- Food: Chocolate, eggplant, black rice, purple cauliflower, purple sweet potato, passion fruit, acai
- Flowers: Gladiolus, dahlia, tulip, ranunculus, stock
- Spices: Cocoa, pepper
- Scents: Wet earth, black tea, pepper
- Crystals and Stones: Topaz, dyed agate, hematite, blue goldstone
- Energy Center: 8 / crown chakra
- Clothing: Anything that's very comfortable

Clear

What I Crave (Future State)

- release of suffering

- movement through sadness

- shedding tears

- understanding why

- seeing the light

- clarity

- optimism

- feeling cleansed

Sample *I am* / Gem Statements

- I can't move past the sadness.

- I need to cry, but can't.

- I don't understand why.

- My life is suffering.

- Nothing is clear to me.

Sample Questions

- What do I need to understand?

- If I never understood why, how could I still come to terms and accept?

- What if this is exactly how my life is supposed to be?

- How does suffering define me?

- Who would I be if I had clarity?

- What moments of clarity have I had?

- What makes me the most optimistic?

- If I felt washed clean, how would I be from now on? How can I be that way anyway?
- Who do I think really needs to forgive me?
- Who would I be if I weren't long-suffering?
- When I am no longer sad, who will I be?
- What if I do know why?
- What gives me light?
- How am I a light worker?

Sample Mantras or Beliefs

- I can let go of my suffering.
- I am not defined by my suffering.
- My tears flow as an expression of my understanding.
- I am moving through the sadness.
- I release what I no longer need.
- I am a lightworker.

Ideas for Using Clear

- Food: Water, broth, tea
- Flowers: Skeleton flower
- Spices: Sea salt
- Scents: Clean, linen, fresh air
- Crystals and Stones: Clear quartz, angel aura, diamond, Herkimer diamond
- Energy: Choose your own—especially using white light
- Clothing: Take a bath, skinny-dip, sleep naked

White

What I Crave (Future State)

- fresh start
- clean slate
- cleansing
- lightness
- handing over the past
- angel wings
- signs
- clouds
- unfettered flight
- working with light

Sample *I am* / Gem Statements

- I feel responsible for so much.
- It's all my fault.
- I'm holding more than I can take.
- I have been so bad.
- I can't hear the messages anymore.

Sample Questions

- How am I responsible?
- What if I'm not responsible?
- What if I'm not responsible anymore?
- How am I so important that it's all my fault?
- Do I ask for signs and messages?
- Am I willing to ask for signs and messages?

- What if the past doesn't matter today?
- Aren't I just human?
- What if I can take it?
- What would I say to the angels or to my guides?
- What messages do I want to hear?
- What if I were surrounded by signs? What would I see?
- What is blocking the light?
- How can I work more with light?
- What if I stop ignoring the signs?
- What do you I in the clouds?
- How do I have everything I need?
- Who is my guardian angel?
- How can I be more like an angel?
- What if I'm already absolutely forgiven and loved?

Sample Mantras or Beliefs

- I am responsible for myself and my own actions.
- I can handle what comes my way.
- I am only and always human.
- I see signs and hear messages—and my understanding grows.
- I listen to my guides.
- I am good.

Ideas for Using White

- Food: rice, popcorn, cauliflower, onion, beans, white fish, yogurt, coconut
- Flowers: plumeria, daisy, white rose, orchid, lily, carnation

- Spices: sage, white pepper, sea salt, horseradish
- Scents: white sage, jasmine, clean
- Crystals and Stones: milky quartz, howlite, moonstone, opal
- Energy: white light—applied locally or encompassing the whole body
- Clothing: anything —especially what's flowing and easy

General Questions

And now for the list of general questions. These are a few of my all-time favorites.

My favorite question right now is this one, which has been the core question of my quarantine experience:

- What is left if/when I take away X?

My favorite trick of all time is to ask these two questions whenever your brain says, *I don't know* (you'll be amazed how often you get an answer— like almost every single time!):

- What if I did know? What would I say?

Here's another great trick, for when you've resorted to *Why?* or *I don't understand*:

- What purpose did this serve?

And here are some more general questions:

- What could make this magical?
- How is this perfect?

- How can I add joy, fun, love, light, (etc.)?
- What little things can I do?
- What can I do today?
- What am I grateful for?
- How can I live my best life?
- How can I use this?
- What can I learn from this?
- What am I making this mean?
- What am I making this mean about me?
- What if it's just not true?
- What if there is nothing wrong?
- What would feel better?
- What evidence do I have about this topic?
- How am I collecting evidence to support my old thoughts?
- What evidence am I ignoring because it doesn't fit my old belief?
- What would change everything? Why?
- Am I making this harder than it is? How? Why or why not?
- How can I make this easy?
- What do I want?
- What do I want to do?
- How do I want to feel?
- What if... the opposite of this?
- How has this served me in the past?
- What if this were no longer true for me?

Remember, there are always more questions on **therainbowonion.com** website.

CHAPTER 15

OTHER WAYS TO USE COLOR THINKING

"Bibliomancy: Divination by jolly well Looking It Up."

—Marilyn Johnson *This Book Is Overdue!: How Librarians and Cybrarians Can Save Us All*

There are more ways to use Color Thinking than the full-on Rainbow Onion process. This chapter gives you a few of those options, but it's not an exhaustive list. I hope you know by now it's completely possible and totally allowable to come up with your own ways to use Color Thinking. If you do, it would be awesome if you'd share. Please post in the comments section on the website!

The Rainbow Onion process is all about working with a layer, then coming across another, deeper layer, which usually means there's a "big thing" to work on, with, or through. (Did you see that? I ended a sentence with THREE prepositions!)

This doesn't have to be a problem. More layers are a sign that a thing—Your Thing—wants reconciliation and transformation. Sometimes, using one (or more) of these other options can help to get you where you want to go.

Ideas for Spot Color Thinking

Color Thinking can be useful for smaller things. I like to call this *spot Color Thinking*. In offset printing, you can apply a single color to a print job instead of printing the whole thing in a full-color process. So instead of doing the full Rainbow Onion process printing, you might only have a small job you need to do. Applying a wee spot of color (you should say that with a British accent, as you would say, "A spot of tea") can sort things out.

Here are a few examples and options for applying a spot of Color Thinking.

Are you stuck? Do you need a nudge to open your mind and get the creative thought-juice flowing?

- Pick the first color that comes into your mind and play with it. Doodle, draw, write.
- Pick a color and look up the questions for it in Chapter 14 to see if they give you a new perspective.
- Look at the color wheel on *The Rainbow Onion* website (or find a color wheel online) and pick two colors exactly opposite from each other. Compare and contrast them. Play with the messages, questions, etc. from Chapter 14 to and see what might open up. Doodle with both colors!

Is a color stalking you? Maybe it's a special message just for you. Try one of these:

- Look up the color in Chapter 14 and see if something in there speaks to you.

- Consider the objects or ways the color is presenting itself to you— is there something about those objects or ways that speaks to you?
- Try color breathing or meditating and see if something comes up for you.
- Journal on one of the questions from Chapter 14 related to the stalker color.

Are you stuck on one specific question?

- Do a reverse look-up! Glance through the questions in Chapter 14 to see if one is similar to the question you're stuck on. What is the color associated with that question? See if something in that color's information opens a door, changes your perspective, or helps you focus on a new question.
- Browse through the blog posts about Color Thinking on *The Rainbow Onion* website to help you decide which color to use, and to find some suggestions on how to use it.
- Clear your mind with white. Answer a few white questions from Chapter 14. Wash yourself with white light.

Do you feel needy without knowing specifics or what color to use? Do you need something, but can't narrow it down to a specific enough feeling or color?

- Browse through the blog posts about Color Thinking on *The Rainbow Onion* website to help you decide on a color to use, and to get some suggestions on how to use it.
- Read through the Future State descriptions in Chapter 14 to see what you're craving. Your description of what you need doesn't

have to be perfect—just pick something that jumps out at you. Pick a color. Look through the information for that color and *do something*. Eat the color, use a fragrance, color breathe, journal, hold a crystal in that color. Pick *something* and indulge yourself. Give yourself something that draws you to it. It will be something you need or want.

Do you want to try using a random way of picking a color? This is like using an oracle card or doing a tarot reading to learn something. You don't even have to have a specific question. There are probably a million ways to draw a random color.

- Close your eyes and point out at the world. Open your eyes and choose the color of a thing you pointed to.
- Make a color wheel with a dial you can spin.
- Make a deck of cards out of color chips from a paint store and pick from the pile.
- Close your eyes and pick from a stash of crayons, pens, or colored pencils.

Do you want to confirm your intuition on something?

- Let your intuition pick a color (or use a random-pick option above). Use that color as intuition confirmation. Look up the color in Chapter 14 for a message or a question.
- Look at our surroundings for the color you're working with. How does it show up? How do you interpret that?
- Ask someone what the color you're working with means to them. Ask them to tell you a Color Thinking Story, for example, and see

what comes up for you about it that ties to what your intuition is telling you.

- Ask for a sign, then look around for it.

Googlemancy

The quotes at the start of the Part 3 introduction and at the start of this chapter are great examples of using a search engine for bibliomancy. I googled "bibliomancy quotes" and chose these two quotes from the results. Because I could.

I would argue that finding things by chance doesn't only *feel* significant, it *is* significant. I would also argue that it's not irrational at all. I really like the quote for this chapter, because I choose to make it mean we have more tools for looking things up at our disposal than we realized.

My favorite thing is a new form of bibliomancy. I could call it *cyberomancy* but I'm going to go with *Googlemancy*.

I like to search for a color online, in Google image search, in Pinterest, or in my own documents—to see what catches my eye or my mind's eye.

Or sometimes I think up an unusual way to use a color in a question that I do a Google search for, like *How does purple cry? Why is green best? Who is orange?* Then I scroll through the search results and chase what I like.

Or I put together a series of random words as they come to me and pop them into the search bar, like *lyrics pink confidence* or *butterfly blue boyfriend*. Then look at the search results. Maybe redo the same search for images, or maybe the videos. I'm often surprised when the entire random phrase I searched for comes up as predictive text—*What?! Someone already searched for this?*

When I do Googlemancy, I feel free to hop down any rabbit hole, take things completely out of context, and look anywhere for meaning. After all, I'm not researching, investigating, fact-checking, or doing anything that requires rigorous accuracy. I am looking for random inspiration and insight. There are no rules other than the one rule: I get to decide the meaning of something that speaks to me.

You should try this if you haven't already!

Doing and Not Doing

By the way, you can use any situation as an excuse—I mean reason—for some quality self-care. It's amazing how you can clean up your thinking or get a fresh perspective or jump-start your creativity or find a sign just by getting outside and walking.

Here's something else really cool. Sometimes, you don't have to DO anything. Sometimes the color will come to you. It might appear right when you need it. It might shine bright, drawing your eyes to an object, place, or person you need to notice.

Sometimes a color will flood your heart. One day, a new color might step up to be your new favorite. Sometimes, a color will haunt you. It will get in your face, in your food, in what you read, in your music; people will be wearing it; it will come in your mail, show up in your social media feed, appear on TV—EVERY-*frickin'*-WHERE—until you pay attention.

You Are the Expert in Charge

Guess what? You're the one who is the expert on interpreting what a color is saying to you. It's your language. You can choose to make a color mean something wonderful. You can choose to let this color be your ally, your support.

Ultimately, this applies to all of Color Thinking: you are in charge. This is your language and you have the right to choose what it all means. You can choose to live in the shadows and the shadow side if you want. But why would you, when you can choose to understand and interpret things as evidence of your new beliefs that support you, serve you, and push you to be your best?

Why wouldn't you choose to align with the light? Since you have the option of choosing, why would you choose anything else?

Now What?

"Books are a uniquely portable magic."

—Stephen King, *On Writing: A Memoir of the Craft*

I love Stephen King's writing. Always have. Yeah, we write in wildly different genres. But, for both of us, good always seems to triumph. You've been working here with this book, which is a form of magic and quite portable. But now you might be wondering what form your magic might take as you use this book to create in your own life.

Now what? Where do you go from here?

I bet you can guess I'm going to say there isn't any one answer (because *yada yada no one size*, etc. *blah dee blah blah*). Well, you'd be right! Where you go from here totally, 100%, absolutely depends on what you want and need.

See if any of these next directions are a fit for you:

Did you read this book and think, *yep, now I'd like to give it a try?*

Awesome. Go back through the book and do the work. And might I recommend you go to the website to get the supporting bonuses and goodies? That will make the journey easier.

Did you read the book and think, *I'd like to play with Color Thinking, but I'm not ready / in the mood / don't have time / don't feel the pull to work on something right now?*

Also awesome. Go to Chapter 15 and check out some of the on-the-spot ways to use Color Thinking and play around with it.

Did you read the book and think, *I'd like to try working with Color Thinking with a small group of friends?*

More awesomeness. Why not start a group and work through *The Rainbow Onion* process together? You can do it like a book club or study group. If you'd like some tips, send me an email. If you think you have a group and want to put together an event or do a retreat about *The Rainbow Onion* process, you could do that. Or we could do that. Again, send me an email.

Did you read the book and do the work and now you're thinking you might want to go deeper?

If so, you have some options. Here are two, for starters: Come to a Rainbow Onion event, or I can coach you one-on-one. For information about events, check out the website to see what's coming up. To find out about one-on-one coaching, go to **therainbowonion.com/coaching** to read about how it works, and we can set up a complimentary call.

***

No matter how you explore Color Thinking and *The Rainbow Onion*, my intention is for you to find your own way to peel the onion of your dreams.

Now What?

I would love to hear about your experience!

Website: **TheRainbowOnion.com**

Email: **Info@TheRainbowOnion.com**

Epilogue

A Letter to You

Dear Beautiful Reader,

If you've made it this far, I feel pretty confident I can be honest with you and tell you a bit more about myself, my story, what really happened to make me write this book, why it did, and what I wish for you. In other words, I want to write you a love letter, and I feel safe enough to be vulnerable and reveal my woo-woo underwear.

I said in the Introduction that I feel like *The Rainbow Onion* is a calling, and that I was pretty much told to write this book and get it out there. Saying "I was told" is putting it mildly. Here's what happened...

A while back, I happened upon an opportunity to do a seven-day retreat in Hawaii. I hadn't done anything like that since my high school church youth group retreat. The topic of the retreat was Living in a Body You Love, which sounded like a pretty cool idea to me, and it was in Hawaii, on the big island. I thought the whole thing sounded wonderful, so I signed up about five months in advance and did all the work to prepare for the event.

I landed in Hawaii in October and was all set for a relaxing, refreshing, rejuvenating experience. The retreat was packed full of amazing, meaningful, and one-of-a-kind experiences. But, as it turned out, they were not the experiences the leader had planned, and my lessons weren't exactly what she had intended.

Someone took over the agenda. *Someone* sent me a whole bunch of signs and symbols. *Pay attention to the sky. Look for feathers. Pay attention to white.*

On the next to last day of the retreat, it became clear to me what was going on.

We all got in a van and headed to Southpoint, the southernmost point in the US and a place where a bunch of ley lines (energy lines) cross. Southpoint is a wide-open grassy plain that pretty much drops off into the ocean. It reminds me of the Bodega headlands in Northern California.

The closer we got to Southpoint, the more pissy I got. I didn't understand why, but I was feeling all kinds of impatience, frustration, and anger.

When we parked, I got out and headed straight for the cliffs, thinking I just needed to get out of the car and get some fresh air.

The air was warm (not hot) and smelled like yeast bread baking in an oven. I *knew* that smell. The sky was clear blue, with a few wispy clouds. It was quite windy, and the clouds blew quickly across the sky—flying. Clouds in the shape of wings.

Angel wings.

Angel wings smell like baking bread.

"MAGGIE, WHAT THE HELL ARE YOU DOING!? GET OFF YOUR ASS!"

The words boomed in my head. I'm cleaning up the language for you here. Not everyone is comfortable with the idea that angels swear. Let me just say, in his defense, this angel pretty much needed to swear to get my attention.

"Stop disrespecting your life and the lessons you've been served up! Quit chasing external certifications. You're stalling! Stop being confused. It's time to heal the timeline. Get this stuff out into the world! Get off your ass and get going!"

I burst out laughing because I recognized that voice. It was Archangel Michael. He had to slap me upside the head and get me back on track. And it worked.

Since that day, I've had enough reminders—I call them maintenance signs—to help me keep a sense of clarity and to prod me to put—and keep—my butt in gear to get this stuff out in the world.

This is what I meant when I say this is my calling: I was pretty much told to share it.

***

So, on to what I wish for you.

I wish for you to become the best version of yourself, and to live the best life you possibly can—however YOU define that.

I hope you will take the time you need to take care of yourself. Know that the better you are—the happier and healthier you are, the more you will be able to give back to your world. It's okay to be happy and strong and healthy. Don't we want that for everyone?

This doesn't have to be hard. Suffering isn't a pre-requisite for change. Struggle doesn't lead to the moral high ground. There is gain without pain.

So I wish you peace. And ease.

I believe in the ripple effect. The better you and I are, the better the world around us will be. The world needs us to be our best. This is how we make a better world.

My wish for you is to become the biggest, best, splashiest rock (a gemstone!) you can be—the you that creates massive ripples when you cannonball into the lake of life.

For me, wishing isn't just passive. We have to do things to make our wishes come true. You have to take some kind of action.

Sharing *The Rainbow Onion* is my action, throwing my colorful onion into the mix.

This is me, tossing this book into the lake and watching the ripples grow.

Love and light,
Maggie

ACKNOWLEDGMENTS

This is my life's work. Yup, it is. Which means I have a lifetime of people to acknowledge here. No pressure, right?

I apologize in advance for all the people I know I don't mention here by name, in words on the page. Please know you are written in my heart.

First, I want to thank my amazing family: The ones who have left—my mom, my brothers, and my grandfather; and the ones who are here now—Katie, Jordan, Madison, Katlyn, Tabitha, Morgan, Danny, and Charlie.

I also want to thank these very special people in my now: Rob Angus Jones, Beth Splizzy Carter, Mitch Matthews, Michele Baroody, Will Toft, Grace Kerina, Lindsay Palmer, the Master Group, Heather Russell, Trinity Houston, Darla LaDoux, Las Peregrinas, and Emily and Jaycee Pickens-Jones.

Thank you to the people who have played a major role in my history (at least the part that got me here): Johnny Silaj, Victoria Silks, Elizabeth Linebarger Clinton, Angela Lauria, Mr. Kruljac, the entire Severson clan, Rita Valois, Michael Kluczko.

And thanks to the music, always the music. I miss the music. I hope that the world can sing together again very soon.

Thank you to everyone who helped by being a beta reader and being on the launch team. You are my village!

ABOUT THE AUTHOR

Maggie Huffman is the founder of *The Rainbow Onion* and Color Thinking. She is an author, coach, and singer. She's also a consultant in the wine industry. Her several previous careers make a colorful patchwork quilt of experiences. She'll readily pull from any of them to make a point, help a client, or mix a metaphor.

Maggie lives in Sonoma, California (hey, someone has to do it!), where if she isn't working or playing in the aforementioned areas, she's filling in the spaces with other random interests. She is (literally) surrounded by her German Shepherd, Nic, and her two cats, Bimfee and Puppy.

Maggie's favorite color is any shade of purple. She stubbornly believes that life is good and that reconciliation and healing are pretty much the same thing.

THANK YOU!

Thank you so much for reading this book. I hope you played with color and peeled your onion. I hope you learned something and that it helped you.

I'd love it if you'd leave an honest review on the retailer you purchased this from. This will help more people find this book. The more reviews a book has, the more relevant the retailer considers it.

Thanks again for your support. It means more than you'll ever know!

Made in the USA
San Bernardino, CA
29 July 2020